SOME LOST STORIES

SARATH KUMAR KALAMATA

To my beloved wife, Alekhya,

Your unwavering support and love have been the guiding light in my journey as a writer. This book is as much yours as it is mine. Your narration of "Between Two Heartbeats" brought life to its essence, and your encouragement gave me the strength to complete this collection. I am forever grateful for your presence in my life—between every heartbeat and beyond.

Contents

Preface

Love is not just about meeting and staying together; sometimes, it is about losing it and finding again in the most unexpected ways. *Some Lost Stories* is a collection of three love stories, each exploring the depths of emotions, the pain of separation, and the beauty of rediscovery.

Every story in this book carries a piece of my heart, woven with the emotions of love, longing, and fate. One of these stories, *Between Two Heartbeats*, holds special significance as it was narrated by my wife, Alekhya, whose insights and emotions brought it to life in a way only she could. Her presence and encouragement have been a guiding force throughout this journey, making this book even more special to me.

Writing this book has been a journey of reflection—on love, on loss, and on the memories that stay with us forever. It is for everyone who has loved and lost, who has waited and hoped, and who believes that sometimes, love finds its way back through a different person at a different time.

I hope these stories touch your heart as deeply as they have touched mine. Thank you everyone for being a part of this journey.

Acknowledgements

Writing this book has been a journey filled with inspiration, encouragement, and love. I would like to express my heartfelt gratitude to those who have played a significant role in shaping my path as a writer. Every person who come into our lives and leave us definitely share a moment. I wish to collect a few people who left their mark in my journey.

First, to **Lord Ram**, whose virtues and ideals continue to inspire me on my journey to becoming a better human being—a path I am still walking.

To my **family**, whose love and unwavering faith in me have shaped the person I am today—thank you for being my foundation and my strength.

To my teachers—**Manimala, Rajeswari, P. Srinivas Rao (Telugu teacher), and Girish Prasad Rath**—your wisdom and guidance have left an everlasting impact on me. You nurtured my love for literature and storytelling, and for that, I am forever grateful.

To my dear friends—**Uday, Srikanth, Suresh and Lokesh** (whose absence is deeply felt, but whose memories live on in my heart)—thank you for always believing in me. **Sushmita**, for creating the beautiful cover design. You truly are an inspiration in adding colours to my book. **Manjeera**, *a friend and an inspiration*, you inspired me in ways I never imagined, pushing me to begin this book and embrace my voice as a writer. Your support, along with the encouragement of my friends (who read my poetry and uplifted my spirit), means the world to me.

And lastly, to my **wife, Alekhya**—my greatest supporter, my love, and my home. You encouraged me when I doubted myself, nourished me with your kindness (and your delicious cooking), and stood by me through every high and low. This book carries a part of you within its pages, just as my heart carries you in every beat.

Prologue

Life is a journey, unpredictable and ever-changing. Some find love in the rush of youth, while others stumble upon it much later—sometimes within the bonds of marriage, and sometimes in the ashes of a love they thought would last forever. Love does not always follow the paths we expect; it has its own way of finding us, often when we least expect it.

The stories in this book revolve around such unexpected love—where hearts meet after marriage or after the loss of a so-called *soulmate*. They explore the beauty of second chances, the resilience of the human heart, and the idea that love is not confined to a single moment or a single person. Some of these events are inspired by real-life experiences of people I have met—strangers who became storytellers, friends who shared their deepest emotions, and souls who found love in ways they never imagined.

This book is a reminder that love is never truly lost; it only takes a different shape, waits in a different corner of time, and finds us when we are ready to embrace it again.

1

he calls me, His Ammu

Not all love stories are loud.

Some exist in quiet corners, in unsaid words, in the space between longing and restraint.

Some love stories aren't meant to be spoken aloud.

Some exist in quiet glances, in unread messages, in the comfort of knowing that someone, somewhere, understands.

This is a story of love that wasn't declared—yet existed more powerfully than words ever could.

The Morning Ritual

The first light of dawn crept into the room like a hesitant guest, brushing the walls with a soft, golden hue. I stirred awake, my body still heavy with sleep, but my mind already drifting to the day ahead. The ceiling fan whirred above, its rhythmic hum a constant companion in the quiet of the morning. I turned my head slightly, my gaze falling on Rohan, lying beside me. He was still asleep, his face serene, his chest rising and falling in a steady rhythm. For a moment, I allowed myself to just watch him—the man I had married, the father of my children, the person who shared my bed but sometimes felt miles away from my heart.

Rohan was handsome in a quiet, unassuming way. His features were sharp, his jawline strong, and his skin bore the faintest trace of stubble that he would shave off later. His hair, always neatly combed, was slightly dishevelled now, a rare glimpse of vulnerability. I wondered if he ever looked at me the way I looked at him—with a mix of love, longing, and a quiet ache for something more.

I slipped out of bed, my feet touching the cold floor, and padded softly to the bathroom. The mirror greeted me with the reflection of a woman who had learned to carry the weight of her emotions with grace. My dark, almond-shaped eyes held a depth of feeling that I rarely let surface. My skin, the colour of warm honey, glowed faintly in the morning light. My lips, naturally tinted a soft rose, curved into a smile that didn't always reach my eyes. I had been told I was beautiful, but beauty, I had learned, was not enough to bridge the gaps between hearts.

The water from the shower was warm, cascading over my skin like a gentle embrace. I closed my eyes, letting it wash away the remnants of sleep. I dressed carefully, choosing a simple yet elegant salwar kameez in a shade of deep blue that complemented my complexion. I tied my long, dark hair into a loose braid, letting a few strands escape to frame my face. There was a quiet pride in the way

I presented myself, a silent rebellion against the mundanity of my days.

By the time I finished my puja, the house was beginning to stir. The scent of incense lingered in the air, mingling with the aroma of freshly brewed coffee. I moved to the kitchen, my sanctuary, where the rituals of cooking grounded me. The sizzle of mustard seeds in hot oil, the soft hiss of curry leaves, the rhythmic chopping of vegetables—these were the sounds of my mornings, the sounds of a life I had built with my own hands.

I woke Taara and Vihaan, their sleepy protests bringing a faint smile to my lips. Taara, my little girl, was the image of her father, with his sharp features and quiet demeanour. Vihaan, my baby boy, was all energy and mischief, his laughter a balm to my soul. "Come on, my loves," I coaxed, brushing Taara's hair and helping Vihaan into his uniform. They were my anchors, my reason to keep going, even on days when the world felt heavy.

Rohan entered the kitchen just as I was setting the table, his presence filling the room with a quiet, familiar energy. He was dressed for work, his crisp white shirt tucked neatly into his trousers, but his tie was slightly askew, as though he had rushed through the final touches of his morning routine. I couldn't help but smile at the sight—it was such a small thing, but it reminded me of the man I had fallen in love with, the man who was always so meticulous yet somehow endearingly imperfect.

I stepped closer to him, my fingers reaching out to adjust his tie. The fabric felt smooth under my touch, but it was the warmth of his chest beneath my fingertips that made my breath catch. For a fleeting moment, I allowed myself to linger, my hand resting lightly against him, hoping he might feel the unspoken words that lingered between us. He looked down at me, his dark eyes meeting mine, and offered a small, polite smile. "Thanks," he said softly, his voice steady but distant, as though he were thanking a stranger for a kind gesture rather than his wife for a moment of intimacy.

I nodded, my own smile faltering slightly as I stepped back. We sat down to eat, the clink of utensils against plates filling the silence that stretched between us like an invisible wall. The table was set with care—steaming idlis, coconut chutney, and a small bowl of sambar, all prepared with the love I poured into every meal. But as I watched him eat, his eyes focused on his plate, I couldn't help but feel the weight of the unspoken words that hung in the air.

It wasn't that we didn't care for each other. We did. We had built a life together, raised two beautiful children, and shared countless moments of joy and struggle. But somewhere along the way, the easy flow of conversation had dried up, replaced by a polite, almost formal exchange of words. I longed for the days when we would talk for hours, when his laughter would fill the room and his eyes would light up with the kind of passion that made me feel like the most important person in his world. Now, it felt as though we were two strangers sharing a meal, bound by routine but separated by an invisible chasm.

I wanted to reach across the table, to take his hand and ask him how he was, really ask him. I wanted to tell him about the ache in my heart, the loneliness that crept in even when he was right beside me. But the words stuck in my throat, held back by the fear of rejection, of hearing him say, "I'm fine," in that same polite tone that told me nothing.

So, I sat there, sipping my coffee and stealing glances at him, hoping he might look up and see the longing in my eyes. But he didn't. He finished his meal, thanked me again, and stood to leave, his mind already elsewhere. As I watched him walk away, I felt the familiar sting of tears behind my eyes, but I blinked them away. There was work to be done, a house to manage, and a life to live. And so, I buried my feelings deep inside, where no one could see them, and carried on with my day, as I always did.

"There's a party this weekend," I said, breaking the quiet. "At the Kapoors'. Should we go?"

Rohan nodded, his eyes on his plate. "Sure, if you want to."

I waited for more—a question, a comment, anything—but nothing came. I tried again. "It might be nice to get out. We haven't been to one in a while."

"Yeah," he said, still not looking up. "It'll be good."

I bit my lip, the familiar ache settling in my chest. Why was it so hard for him to talk to me? To really talk? I wanted to ask him, to tell him how much it hurt, but the words stuck in my throat. Instead, I forced a smile and nodded. "I'll let them know we're coming."

The rest of the morning passed in a blur. I packed the kids' lunches, kissed them goodbye, and watched as Rohan drove them to school. The house was quiet again, the silence pressing against my skin. I cleaned up the kitchen, the motions automatic, my mind elsewhere.

By mid-morning, I was at my desk, my laptop opens in front of me. Work was my escape, my sanctuary. As a social media manager, I handled high-profile clients, crafting posts and strategies that kept their brands alive. It was a job I was good at, one that gave me a sense of purpose. The money I earned was more than just a contribution to the household; it was my way of staying connected to my parents back in India. Every month, I sent them a portion of my earnings, a small token of gratitude for all they had done for me.

Rohan was proud of me, I knew that. He often told me how much he admired my dedication; how happy he was that I had found something I loved. But admiration wasn't enough. I wanted more—more of him, more of us.

I immersed myself in my work, the glow of the screen a distraction from the emptiness I felt. The hours passed; the house quiet except for the occasional ping of a notification. It was a life I had chosen, a life I had built, but sometimes, in the stillness of the afternoon, I couldn't help but wonder—was this all there was?

The pain was always there, a quiet undercurrent beneath the surface of my days. It wasn't the sharp, searing pain of betrayal or loss, but a dull, persistent ache that never quite went away. It was in the way Rohan's eyes would slide away from mine when I tried to talk to him, in the way he would nod and smile but never really engage. It was in the way I longed for him to reach out, to hold me, to tell me he loved me in a way that felt real and true.

I had tried, in the early years of our marriage, to bridge the gap between us. I had tried to make him laugh, to draw him out of his shell, to show him that I was here, that I was his. But no matter what I did, he remained distant, his emotions locked away behind a wall I couldn't penetrate. Eventually, I had stopped trying, not because I didn't care, but because it hurt too much to keep reaching for something that wasn't there.

And yet, I loved him. I loved him for the man he was, for the father he was to our children, for the life we had built together. But sometimes, love wasn't enough. Sometimes, I wanted more—more than the polite smiles, the quiet dinners, the distant affection. I wanted the passion, the connection, the intimacy that I had always dreamed of.

The day stretched on, the sun climbing higher in the sky. I worked, I cooked, I cleaned, I waited. For what, I wasn't sure. But deep down, I knew I was waiting for something to change.

The Unexpected Connection

It began on an ordinary day, much like any other. The kids were at school, Rohan was at work, and I was sitting at my desk, scrolling through Facebook during a break between client meetings. A notification popped up—a friend request from someone named Shannu. The name didn't ring a bell, but his profile picture caught my attention. He had a warm smile, his eyes crinkling at the corners, and an air of quiet confidence about him. Curious, I clicked on his profile.

Shannu was a writer, his bio said. His timeline was filled with thoughtful posts—quotes, reflections on life, and snippets of his writing. There was something about the way he expressed himself that drew me in. I accepted the request, and within minutes, a message popped up.

Shannu: Hi Manjula! I hope you don't mind me reaching out. I just realized we're from the same hometown. Small world, isn't it?

I smiled, typing back.

Manjula: Hi Shannu! No, I don't mind at all. It's always nice to connect with someone from back home. How do you know me?

Shannu: We're form the same town, though I doubt you'd never seen me. I was one of those quiet kids who stayed in the background. But I remember you. You were hard to miss.

His words made me pause. There was a hint of something in his tone—something nostalgic, almost wistful.

Manjula: That's sweet of you to say. I'm afraid I don't remember much from those days. Life has been a whirlwind since then.

Shannu: I can imagine. You've built quite a life for yourself. I've seen your posts—you're doing amazing work.

We chatted for a while that day, exchanging pleasantries and sharing a bit about our lives. It was easy, effortless, and by the end of the conversation, I found myself looking forward to hearing from him again.

ppp

A few days later, Shannu messaged me again.

Shannu: How's your day going, Manjula?

I glanced at the clock. It was mid-afternoon, and I was in the middle of preparing lunch for the kids, who would be home soon.

Manjula: Busy, as usual. Just finished some work and now getting lunch ready. How about you?

Shannu: Same here. Writing can be all-consuming, but I love it. By the way, I read one of your recent posts about balancing work and family. You have a way with words.

I smiled, stirring the curry on the stove as I typed.

Manjula: Thank you. It's not easy, but I try my best. What about you? What inspires your writing?

Shannu: Life, mostly. People, their stories, their emotions. I've always been fascinated by how complex yet beautiful human connections can be.

His words resonated with me, and before I knew it, we were discussing everything from our favourite books to our philosophies on life.

Shannu: You know, I had a crush on you back in the day you're in the town.

I blinked at the screen, surprised by his candour.

Manjula: Really? I had no idea.

Shannu: Of course not. I was too shy to ever say anything. But you were always so confident, so full of life. It was hard not to notice you.

I laughed, feeling a strange mix of flattery and nostalgia.

Manjula: Well, I'm glad we're connecting now. Better late than never, right?

Shannu: Absolutely.

ᗡᗡᗡ

It happened during one of our late-night conversations, the kind where the world outside seemed to fade away, leaving only the glow of the screen and the warmth of their words. Shannu had been teasing me about something trivial—my love for overly sweet chai or the way I always organized my desk with military precision. I laughed, my fingers flying over the keyboard to fire back a witty reply.

Manjula: You're one to talk! I've seen your workspace in your videos. It's chaos incarnate.

Shannu: Chaos? That's where the magic happens, Ammu.

She paused, her breath catching at the unfamiliar yet endearing name.

Manjula: Ammu? Where did that come from?

Shannu: I don't know. It just feels right. You're strong, but there's this softness to you too. Ammu suits you.

For a moment, she didn't know how to respond. It was such a small thing, a simple pet name, but it carried a weight she hadn't expected. It felt intimate, like a secret shared between just the two of them.

Manjula: I like it.

Shannu: Good. Because I'm not taking it back.

From that day on, "Ammu" became his name for her, a quiet reminder of the bond they shared—one that was growing deeper with every conversation.

ᐁᐁᐁ

One evening, after a particularly exhausting day, I logged into Facebook to find a message from Shannu.

Shannu: You've been quiet today. Everything okay?

I hesitated, surprised by how perceptive he was.

Manjula: Just a long day. The kids were being difficult, and work was overwhelming.

Shannu: I can tell. Your texts usually have a certain energy to them. Today, they feel heavier.

His observation caught me off guard.

Manjula: You're very perceptive.

Shannu: It's part of being a writer, I guess. We notice the little things. Do you want to talk about it?

I sighed, glancing at the pile of laundry waiting to be folded.

Manjula: Not really. It's just one of those days where everything feels like too much.

Shannu: I get that. Sometimes, it's okay to feel overwhelmed. You don't always have to be strong; you know.

His words were kind, but I wasn't ready to let my guard down.

Manjula: I'll be fine. Just need to get through the evening.

Shannu: If you say so. But remember, it's okay to lean on someone every once in a while.

ᗁᗁᗁ

A few weeks later, we were chatting late in the afternoon after the kids had gone to school. The house was quiet, the kind of quiet that felt rare and precious. I was sitting at my desk, a cup of tea cooling beside me, when Shannu's message popped up on the screen.

Shannu: Do you ever think about the past?

I leaned back in my chair, considering his question. The past was a strange thing—sometimes it felt like a distant memory, and other times, it felt like it was just yesterday.

Manjula: Sometimes. Mostly about how much has changed. Why do you ask?

There was a pause before his reply came through, as though he was choosing his words carefully.

Shannu: I was thinking about my teenage years. I was such a dreamer back then, always lost in my thoughts.

I smiled, imagining a younger version of him—quiet, introspective, and perhaps a little unsure of himself.

Manjula: Sounds like you haven't changed much.

He laughed, and I could almost hear the warmth in his voice through the screen.

Shannu: Maybe not. But back then, I used to have this huge crush on someone. It was all-consuming, though I never had the courage to tell her.

I felt a pang of curiosity, mixed with something else—something I couldn't quite name.

Manjula: What happened to her?

There was a longer pause this time, and I could almost feel the weight of his thoughts.

Shannu: Life happened. We went our separate ways. But I've always wondered what might have been if I'd been braver.

His words lingered in my mind, but before I could respond, he sent another message.

Shannu: Actually, there's more to it. A few years ago, I was in a serious relationship. I thought she was the one. We were together for three years, and I truly believed we'd build a life together.

I sat up a little straighter, sensing the shift in his tone.

Manjula: What happened?

Shannu: I wasn't ready. Not in the way she needed me to be. I was still figuring things out—my career, my finances, my place in the world. She wanted stability, a future, and I couldn't give that to her at the time.

I could feel the ache in his words, the regret that came with hindsight.

Manjula: That must have been hard.

Shannu: It was. I tried to keep the relationship going, to convince her to wait for me, but she wasn't ready to take that risk. She left, and it broke me for a while.

I felt a lump form in my throat, imagining the pain he must have gone through.

Manjula: I'm so sorry, Shannu. That's a lot to carry.

Shannu: It is. But it's also taught me a lot. About love, about timing, about what it means to be ready for someone.

I hesitated for a moment, then typed my response.

Manjula: You're a good person, Shannu. Anyone would be lucky to have you in their life.

There was a pause, and then his reply came through.

Shannu: Thank you, Ammu. That means a lot coming from you.

I smiled, though there was a bittersweetness to it.

Manjula: You've come so far since then. You're a writer, a thinker, someone who understands people in a way not many do. That's something to be proud of.

Shannu: I don't know about that. But I do know that I've learned to appreciate the connections I have now. Like this one.

His words made my heart skip a beat, but I quickly pushed the feeling aside.

Manjula: I'm glad we reconnected too. You've been a good friend, Shannu.

Shannu: And you've been a light in my life, Ammu. More than you know. And more than a friend.

The conversation ended soon after, but his words stayed with me. As I sat there, the afternoon light streaming through the windows, I realized how much Shannu had come to mean to me. He was more than just a friend—he was someone who understood me in a way few others did.

And though I would never admit it out loud, I was grateful for the connection we had found. It was a reminder that even in the midst of life's challenges, there were moments of clarity, of connection, that made everything feel a little less overwhelming.

ᐅᐅᐅ

One afternoon, during a rare moment of quiet, Shannu sent me a video call request. I was sitting in the living room, a cup of tea in hand, the house unusually still after the chaos of the morning. The kids were at school, Rohan was at work, and for the first time in what felt like weeks, I had a moment to myself. When I saw Shannu's name pop up on the screen, I hesitated for only a second before accepting.

His face appeared on the screen, his warm smile instantly putting me at ease. "Hey," he said, his voice soft but filled with a familiarity that made it feel like we'd known each other for years rather than weeks.

"Hey," I replied, smiling back. "What's up?"

"Just wanted to see your face," he said simply, his eyes crinkling at the corners. "You've been on my mind."

I felt a flutter in my chest, a sensation I hadn't felt in a long time, but I quickly brushed it aside. "That's sweet of you," I said, taking a sip of my tea. "I'm just here, trying to keep up with everything. You know how it is."

He nodded, his expression thoughtful. "I do. But sometimes, I wonder how you manage it all. You're like this force of nature—juggling work, family, and still finding time to be there for everyone else."

I laughed, though his words struck a chord. "I don't know about that. Most days, it feels like I'm just barely keeping my head above water."

"Maybe," he said, leaning back in his chair. "But even so, you make it look effortless. I've always admired that about you."

There was a pause, and for a moment, we just looked at each other, the silence comfortable but charged with something unspoken.

"Do you ever think about how much life has changed?" I asked, breaking the quiet. "I mean, back in school, I never would have imagined I'd be here, living this life."

Shannu smiled, a hint of nostalgia in his eyes. "All the time. Back then, I was this shy kid with big dreams but no idea how to make them happen. And you—you were this confident, radiant person who seemed like you had it all figured out."

I shook my head, laughing softly. "I didn't have anything figured out. I was just good at pretending."

"Maybe," he said, his tone gentle. "But even so, you inspired me. I used to watch you from afar, wondering what it would be like to have even a fraction of your confidence."

His words surprised me, and I felt a warmth spread through me. "I had no idea you felt that way."

"Of course not," he said, grinning. "I was too busy trying to blend into the background. But life has a funny way of bringing people back together, doesn't it?"

"It does," I agreed, my mind drifting to the twists and turns that had led me to this moment. "Sometimes, I wonder if I've made the right choices. If I've done enough, been enough."

Shannu's expression softened, and he leaned closer to the screen. "You have, Ammu. You've built this incredible life, and you've done it all with so much grace. But even the strongest people need someone to lean on."

I looked at him, his eyes filled with an understanding that made me feel seen in a way I hadn't in years. It was as if he could see past the mask I wore, past the strength I projected to the world, and straight into the heart of me.

"Thank you, Shannu," I said softly, my voice barely above a whisper. "That means a lot."

He smiled, his gaze steady. "Anytime. You don't have to carry everything alone, you know. I'm here."

Echoes of the Past

Life had settled into a rhythm, a steady cadence of routines and responsibilities. My days were filled with work, the kids, and the occasional conversation with Rohan. We had found a kind of equilibrium, a quiet understanding that allowed us to coexist without too much friction. The longing for more—more affection, more connection—hadn't disappeared, but I had learned to accept what we had. Rohan was a good man, a devoted father, and a reliable partner. He wasn't the romantic hero I had once dreamed of, but he was mine, and that was enough.

Shannu, on the other hand, was becoming a constant presence in my life. Our conversations, once light and casual, had deepened into something more. Some days, they were filled with laughter and teasing; other days, they were tinged with a quiet intensity that left me breathless. He had a way of drawing me out, of making me feel seen in a way I hadn't in years.

One evening, after the kids were in bed and Rohan was engrossed in a cricket match, Shannu and I found ourselves talking late into the night. The conversation had taken a serious turn, as it often did these days.

Shannu: You've never really talked about your past relationships. I feel like I know so much about you, but there's this one part of your life that's still a mystery.

I hesitated, my fingers hovering over the keyboard. The past was a place I rarely visited, not because I didn't want to, but because it still carried a weight that was hard to bear.

Manjula: There's not much to tell. It was a long time ago.

Shannu: I don't believe that. You're not the kind of person who does anything halfway. If you loved someone, it must have been something extraordinary.

His words struck a chord, and before I could stop myself, I began to type.

Manjula: His name was David.

David and I met in college, during our first year. He was tall, with a smile that could light up a room, and a confidence that drew people to him like moths to a flame. I was shy back then, more comfortable with books than with people, but David had a way of making me feel like I was the only person in the world.

Our love story began slowly, with stolen glances and shy smiles, but it didn't take long for it to blossom into something all-consuming. We were inseparable, spending hours talking about everything and nothing. He would surprise me with little gifts—a book he thought I'd like, a single rose he picked on his way to class—and I would write him letters, pouring my heart onto the page.

One evening, as the sun dipped below the horizon, painting the sky in shades of orange and pink, David took my hand and led me to the college rooftop. The city stretched out before us, a sea of lights and possibilities.

"Manju," he said, his voice soft but steady, "I don't know what the future holds, but I know I want you in it. I love you."

Tears filled my eyes as I looked at him, his face illuminated by the fading light. "I love you too," I whispered, my heart swelling with a joy I had never known before.

Theirs was a love story whispered about in the corridors of their college, a tale of stolen glances under monsoon rains and promises sealed behind library shelves. David, with his ink-stained hands and a smile that could thaw winter, had carved a place in Manjula's heart deeper than she ever imagined possible. For two years, they were inseparable—sneaking out to late-night chats, scribbling letters in margins of textbooks, dreaming of a future where caste and culture wouldn't dictate their hearts.

But love, when it burns too brightly, casts shadows.

Manjula's father, a man of traditions and a temper as sharp as a sickle, discovered their secret one humid afternoon. A folded love letter, slipped carelessly from her bag, became the spark that ignited his fury. He stormed into her room, his face a storm cloud, waving the paper like a verdict.

*"You've shamed us!" he roared, his voice shaking the framed gods on the wall. "Do you want to bury me alive?" Manjula pleaded, her tears pooling at her feet, but her father's threats escalated like a monsoon flood. "If you don't end this," he hissed, gripping her wrist, "*You'll see your father's dead body."*

That night, beneath a sky smothered by stars, Manjula met David at their usual spot—the broken bench under the banyan tree. His face lit up when he saw her, but it faded as she stepped back, her voice brittle. "We need to end this." David froze, his laugh dying mid-breath. "What are you saying?" he asked, reaching for her hand. She yanked it away. "My father knows. He'll... he'll kill himself if I don't leave you." David's eyes widened, desperation clawing into his words. "Let me talk to him. Let me explain—" "No!" she snapped, her voice cracking. "You'll make it worse. Just... forget me."

He begged, his voice raw. "Manju, please. One last day. Let me love you one last time, and I'll let you go." His tears mirrored hers, but fear paralyzed her—fear of her father's wrath, of society's scorn, of her own crumbling resolve. She turned away, her silence louder than any goodbye.

The next morning, David stood outside her house, his eyes swollen, clutching a single jasmine flower. Manjula watched from behind curtains, her nails digging into her palms. When her father's shadow darkened the porch, David left, the flower wilting on the doorstep.

Manjula stood motionless, her gaze anchored to the receding figure of David until he dissolved into the horizon's blur—a shadow swallowed by the indifferent dusk. It was as though the ground beneath her fissured, splitting her soul from her body, leaving her hollow, a vessel of ash. Tears carved rivers down her cheeks, not the fiery wrath of lava but the cold, ceaseless drip of monsoon rain—each drop etching scars into her skin, indelible as ink on parchment.

Her dreams, once vivid tapestries woven with threads of stolen laughter and whispered futures, unravelled in an instant. They fell like glass shards, glittering briefly before burying themselves in the earth, too shattered to piece back together. The colours of her world bled out—the cerulean of his eyes, the gold of their sunlit afternoons, the emerald of promises unkept—all faded to a pallid grey, as if life itself had been drained of its pigments.

She remained there, rooted to the spot long after he vanished. The air grew thick with the silence of endings, heavy with the weight of words unsaid. Once, she had been a butterfly—vibrant, unbound, wings painted with the hues of hope. Now, she stood as a relic of that creature, her wings moth-eaten and frayed, every flutter a whisper of what might have been.

The world moved on, but Manjula lingered in the memories, a portrait her love. David did not look back. And the girl who had loved him? She folded herself into the quiet, a symphony unfinished, forever suspended between a chord and its echo.

Their story became a relic, buried under duty and time, but in the monsoons, the tree where they used to meet, still wept.

ﷺﷺﷺ

The final blow came when my marriage was arranged to Rohan. I remember the day my parents told me, their faces stern but their eyes filled with a sadness they couldn't hide.

"It's for the best," my mother said, her voice trembling. "You'll understand one day."

I didn't understand. I couldn't. All I knew was that my heart was breaking, shattering into a million pieces.

David and I met one last time, in the same spot where he had first told me he loved me. The sky was overcast, the air heavy with the promise of rain.

"I can't do this," I said, my voice breaking. "I can't fight them anymore."

David's eyes were filled with tears, but he nodded, his jaw clenched in an effort to hold himself together. "I know," he said softly. "I just want you to be happy."

We held each other for what felt like an eternity, our tears mingling as the first drops of rain began to fall. And then, without another word, we walked away, our paths diverging for the last time.

ᗡᗡᗡ

As I typed out the story, tears streamed down my face, blurring the screen. It had been years since I had allowed myself to think about David, to remember the love we had shared and the pain of losing it.

Manjula: I haven't talked about this in so long. It still hurts, even after all these years.

Shannu's response came quickly, his words filled with a tenderness that made my heart ache.

Shannu: Ammu, I can't imagine how hard that must have been for you. To love someone so deeply and then lose them... it's one of the hardest things anyone can go through.

I wiped my tears, my fingers trembling as I typed.

Manjula: I thought I would never get over him. But life goes on, doesn't it?

Shannu: It does. But that doesn't mean what you had wasn't real. Your love for David, his love for you—it's a part of who you are. And it's beautiful, even if it ended.

His words brought a fresh wave of tears, but also a sense of relief. For the first time in years, I felt like someone truly understood the depth of what I had lost.

Manjula: Thank you, Shannu. For listening, for understanding.

Shannu: Always, Ammu. Always.

As the conversation ended, I sat in the quiet of the night, the weight of the past pressing down on me. But for the first time in a long time, I didn't feel alone. Shannu had seen me, truly seen me, and in that moment, it was enough.

As I rested on the pillow, I remembered a moment from something that we had always stored in our hearts.

ﰯﰯﰯ

It was a perfect summer evening, the kind where the air was warm but not heavy, and the sky was painted in hues of gold and pink as the sun dipped below the horizon. The college campus was quiet, most students having retreated to their hostel or the library, but David and I had slipped away to our favourite spot—a secluded corner of the campus garden, hidden behind a canopy of blooming jasmine vines.

David had been unusually quiet all day, his usual easy smile replaced by a look of quiet determination. I had asked him if something was wrong, but he had just shake his head and said, "I'll tell you later."

Now, as we sat on the old wooden bench, the scent of jasmine filling the air, he turned to me, his eyes searching mine.

"Manju," he began, his voice soft but steady, "there's something I need to tell you."

My heart skipped a beat, but I nodded, urging him to continue.

He took a deep breath, his hands reaching for mine. "I've been trying to find the right words all day, but now that I'm here with you, I realize there are no words big enough to say what I feel. So I'll just say it plainly: I love you. I love you more than I've ever loved anyone or anything in my life. Not even you family nor anyone who comes into your life can love you the way I does."

His words hung in the air, and for a moment, I couldn't breathe.

"You're the first thing I think about when I wake up and the last thing on my mind before I fall asleep," he continued, his voice growing stronger. "When I'm with you, the world feels brighter, like everything is exactly as it should be. And when you're not with me, I feel like a part of me is missing."

Tears filled my eyes, but I didn't try to stop them.

"I love the way you laugh, the way your eyes light up when you're excited about something," he said, his thumb brushing away a tear that had escaped down my cheek. "I love the way you care about people, even when they don't deserve it. I love the way you see the world, with so much hope and kindness. I really, really love the way you look into the world and your eyes, they hold a miracle. They show me everything I could have and those that I lost. They show me my soul. I find a home in them. I love your eyes a lot more than I can ever love you. And most importantly, I love the way you look at me, as if I'm the thing you only care for in the whole world. You make me want to be better, to do better, just so I can be worthy of you."

His words were like a balm to my soul, healing wounds I hadn't even realized were there.

"David," I whispered, my voice trembling.

"I don't know what the future holds," he said, his eyes never leaving mine. "But I know I want you in it. I want to wake up next to you every morning and fall asleep with you in my arms every night. I want to build a life with you, a life filled with love and laughter and all the little moments that make life worth living."

He reached into his pocket and pulled out a small, intricately carved wooden box. Inside was a delicate silver bracelet, its surface etched with tiny flowers.

"This is for you," he said, his voice soft but filled with emotion. "It's not much, but it's a promise. A promise that no matter what happens, I'll always love you. That I'll always be here for you, in whatever way you need me."

I looked at the bracelet, then back at him, my heart overflowing with love.

"David," I said, my voice breaking. "I love you too. More than anything."

He smiled, a smile so bright it could have rivalled the setting sun, and slipped the bracelet onto my wrist. As his fingers brushed against my skin, I felt a shiver run through me, a feeling of completeness I had never known before.

We sat there for what felt like hours, wrapped in each other's arms, the world around us fading away. In that moment, there was no past, no future, just the two of us and the love that bound us together.

It was a love that lit the world, a love that would stay with me long after the sun had set and the stars had taken its place.

A few drops of tears had escaped my eyes and along with them, the memories faded for the night. A new day had begun and my life had started again.

A darkness that always hangs

The months rolled by, and my conversations with Shannu became a cherished part of my daily routine. They were a mix of laughter, teasing, and moments of quiet intimacy that made me feel alive in a way I hadn't in years. Shannu had a way of making even the most mundane days feel special, and I found myself looking forward to our chats more than I cared to admit.

One evening, after the kids were asleep and Rohan was engrossed in a sports match with his friends, I found myself alone with my thoughts. The house was quiet, the kind of quiet that made it easy to get lost in your own mind. I opened my laptop, and as if on cue, a message from Shannu popped up.

Shannu: Hey Ammu, how was your day?

I smiled, my fingers flying over the keyboard.

Manjula: Same as always. Busy but good. How about you?

Shannu: Can't complain. Just finished writing for the day. Feels good to get the words out.

We chatted for a while, exchanging jokes and teasing each other as usual. But then, as the conversation deepened, I felt a familiar weight settle in my chest. There was something I had been avoiding, something I had never shared with anyone. But with Shannu, it felt different. He had a way of making me feel safe, like I could tell him anything.

Manjula: There's something I've never told you. Something I've tried to forget.

There was a pause before his reply came through.

Shannu: You know you can tell me anything, Ammu. Whatever it is, I'm here.

I took a deep breath, my fingers trembling as I typed.

Manjula: There was someone... someone I never wanted to remember or talk about. His name was Cyrus.

The name felt heavy on my tongue, like a secret I had buried deep within myself.

Shannu: Cyrus? What happened?

I hesitated, the memories flooding back despite my best efforts to keep them at bay.

Manjula: He was a gully boy, someone with a bad reputation in our town. He was known for his drug habits and his rough demeanour. I never wanted anything to do with him, but he... he had other plans.

Shannu's response was immediate.

Shannu: What do you mean?

I closed my eyes, the images of those years flashing before me.

Manjula: He proposed to me, Shannu. Out of nowhere. I was just a teenager, and he was this guy who everyone was vexed of. I rejected him, of course. I didn't want anything to do with him. But he didn't take no for an answer.

The words poured out of me, each one carrying the weight of the fear and frustration I had felt back then.

Manjula: For years, he followed me. Everywhere I went, he was there, watching me, waiting for me. He would show up at my college, at the market, even outside my house. He kept asking me to love him back, to give him a chance. But I couldn't. I didn't want to.

Tears streamed down my face as I typed, the memories overwhelming me.

Manjula: I was so scared, Shannu. I didn't know what to do. I told my parents, but they didn't take it seriously. They thought it was just a phase, that he would get tired and leave me alone. But he didn't.

Shannu's response came quickly, his words filled with a quiet anger.

Shannu: Ammu, I'm so sorry you had to go through that. No one should have to live in fear like that.

I wiped my tears, my fingers trembling as I continued.

Manjula: It went on for years. I felt like I was trapped, like there was no way out. I started avoiding places I used to love, just to stay away from him. It was like he had taken over my life without my consent.

There was a long pause before Shannu's next message.

Shannu: What happened then? Did he ever stop?

I took a deep breath, the memories of that time still vivid in my mind.

Manjula: Eventually, he did. But not because he wanted to. He got into some job in a different city, and I think he had to leave town. I never saw him again after that. But the fear... it stayed with me for a long time. After my marriage, he did contact me once. He talked a lot about me and apologised for what he had done to me. Apologies never clear the clouds of fear. I forgave him but the impact was still hanging like a cloud in the clear sky.

Shannu's response was filled with a tenderness that made my heart ache.

Shannu: Ammu, I can't imagine how hard that must have been for you. But you're so strong. You've come so far since then. Now you're a woman with a lot of strength. I guess you can handle the past by making peace with it. Always remember, what's gone is gone forever.

I smiled through my tears, his words bringing a sense of comfort I hadn't realized I needed.

Manjula: Thank you, Shannu. For listening, for understanding.

Shannu: Always, Ammu. Always.

There was a pause, and then he added,

Shannu: You don't have to carry this with you anymore. It's in the past. Leave it there. You've built a beautiful life for yourself, and you deserve to be happy.

His words were like a relief to my tensed heart, soothing the wounds that had never fully healed.

Manjula: I know. And I'm trying. But sometimes, it's hard to forget.

Shannu: You don't have to forget, Ammu. Just don't let it define you. You're so much more than what happened to you.

I nodded, even though he couldn't see me.

Manjula: Thank you, Shannu. For everything.

Shannu: Anytime, Ammu. Anytime.

As the conversation ended, I sat in the quiet of the night, the weight of the past pressing down on me. But for the first time in a long time, I felt a sense of peace. Shannu had seen me, truly seen me, and in that moment, it was enough.

One the bed before falling asleep, I was filled with ambiguity. Unsure of what's going on in my mind. I opened my diary and filled it with everything I can to empty my mind.

Dear Dairy,

I don't know where to begin. My heart feels like it's caught in a storm, swirling with emotions I can't quite name. Shannu... Shannu has become such a significant part of my life, and I don't know how to make sense of it all.

*I like him. No, that's not strong enough. I *love* him. There, I've said it. It feels strange to write it down, to admit it even to myself. But it's true. Shannu has a way of making me feel seen, understood, and valued in a way I haven't felt in years. His words, his presence, his kindness—it's like a relief to my silenced soul, soothing the cracks I didn't even realize were there.*

But here's the thing: I can't let myself cross the line. I won't. I'm married, and no matter how much I care for Shannu, I have a life, a family, responsibilities that I can't—and won't—walk away from. Rohan may not be the hero of my life, but he's my husband, the father of my children, and a good man in his own way. I made a commitment to him, and I intend to honour it.

And yet, Shannu... he makes me feel alive in a way I haven't felt in so long. Our conversations are filled with laughter, teasing, and moments of quiet intimacy that make my heart ache. He understands me in a way no one else does. He sees the parts of me that I've hidden away, the parts I thought no one would ever care to notice.

Sometimes, I wonder what it would be like if things were different. If I were free to love him without guilt or hesitation. But that's not my reality, and I can't let myself dwell on what-ifs. It's not fair to Rohan, to my children, or even to Shannu.

I know Shannu cares for me too. I can see it in the way he talks to me, the way he listens, the way he calls me "Ammu" like it's the most natural thing in the world. But he's never pushed me, never asked for more than I can give. He respects my boundaries, even when I'm not sure where they lie. And for that, I'm grateful.

Still, there are moments when I feel torn. Moments when I want to tell him everything, to let myself fall completely into the warmth of his affection. But I can't. I won't. I have to remind myself of who I am, of the life I've built, of the promises I've made.

Shannu is a gift, a light in my life that I didn't know I needed. But he's also a reminder of the complexities of love, of how it can be both beautiful and painful at the same time. I care for him deeply, but I know that love isn't always about holding on. Sometimes, it's about letting go, about cherishing what you have without trying to make it something it can't be.

So, for now, I'll hold onto the moments we share—the laughter, the conversations, the quiet understanding. I'll let myself feel the joy he brings me, but I won't let it consume me. I'll love him in the way I can, from a distance, without crossing the boundaries that keep me grounded.

Because that's who I am. That's the life I've chosen. And no matter how much my heart may ache, I won't let myself forget that.

Yours,

Manju, otherwise call me **His Ammu**

That night, Manjula's heart rested in quiet peace. She had found someone who not only understood her nightmares but embraced them without judgment. As she thought of David, a familiar warmth filled her heart—a gentle affection that time had never dimmed. A cherished memory surfaced, and her eyes, glistening with nostalgia, whispered a silent hello to her most treasured secret.

The college cricket field buzzed with the chaos of victory. David's team had just clinched the inter-college trophy, and his friends hoisted him onto their shoulders, chanting his name as if he'd single-handedly won the match. His laughter echoed across the grass, bright and unguarded, but Manjula's eyes snagged on what no one else noticed—the smear of dried blood on his left knee, seeping through his white trousers.

She stood at the edge of the crowd, textbooks clutched to her chest, her gaze fixed on that crimson streak. **He's hurt**, *she thought, her stomach tightening. But the revelry swallowed her voice. Boys slapped David's back, girls giggled and vied for his attention, and the moment slipped away like sand through fingers.*

That evening, Manjula sat on the couches, the bloodstain haunting her thoughts. At dawn, she mustered courage and dialled the number she'd coaxed from a mutual friend.

"Hello?" David's voice was groggy, tinged with confusion.

"Hi... I'm Manjula. From the CSE department!! I... I saw you hurt your knee. At the match." Silence stretched, and she rushed on, "I just wanted to make sure you're okay."

A pause. Then, a soft chuckle. "You called at 7 p.m. to ask about a scratch?"

"It wasn't a scratch. There was blood."

The line went quiet. When he spoke again, his tone had softened. "You're the first person who noticed."

She heard the rustle of bedsheets, imagined him sitting up, running a hand through his hair. "It was from a dive to save a boundary. Stupid, really."

"Not stupid. Brave."

Another pause. "You're... different, Manjula."

She bit her lip, her heartbeat a wild drum. "Is that bad?"

"No," he said, and she could hear the smile in his voice. "It's interesting."

That single word—interesting—unspooled into hours of talk. About cricket, books, his fear of failure, her love for old songs. By midnight, the bloodstain was forgotten.

But the **hello**? It became the first thread of a story neither could untangle.

The next day morning, David came to the CSE Department to thank Manjula. He asked about her to one of his friends'. He pointed him towards her.

"There!!", he whispered and took a step forward. She stood up with a tense on her face.

David thought to himself, "She made every other girl unattractive", took a step closer to her and said, "Hi Manju!!"

It's the moment when a thousand miracles await their grand reveal...

Reunion in Homeland

The days leading up to our trip to India were a whirlwind of activity. Packing for a family of four was no small feat, especially with two young children who seemed to outgrow their clothes overnight. Taara, my little girl, was excited about seeing her grandparents, while Vihaan, was more interested in the plane ride itself.

Rohan, as always, was calm and collected, handling the luggage with his usual efficiency. He had taken care of the tickets, the visas, and even the gifts for our families. I appreciated his practicality, even if it sometimes felt like he was more focused on the details than the emotions behind the trip.

As I folded clothes and packed snacks for the kids, my mind kept drifting to Shannu. We had been talking for months, sharing our thoughts, our dreams, and even our fears. But this would be the first time we would meet in person. The thought filled me with a mix of excitement and nervousness.

The day of the journey arrived, and we made our way to the airport. The kids were buzzing with excitement, their chatter filling the car as Rohan drove. I sat in the passenger seat, my mind racing with thoughts of what lay ahead.

The flight was long, but the kids handled it surprisingly well. Taara spent most of the time drawing, while Vihaan was content with his tablet. Rohan and I exchanged a few words, but for the most part, we were lost in our own thoughts.

As the plane lifted into the air, a wave of emotions washed over me. The familiar sights and sounds of my homeland brought a sense of comfort and belonging, but they also stirred a deep longing for the family and friends I had left behind. My parents, my siblings, the streets I had grown up on—they all called to me, filling my heart with a bittersweet nostalgia. I missed the laughter of my childhood friends, the warmth of my mother's embrace, and the comforting presence of my father. These were the ties that bound me to this place, the roots that grounded me no matter how far I travelled.

And yet, in a quiet corner of my heart, there was another longing—a longing to see Shannu. The thought of finally meeting him in person filled me with a mix of excitement and nervousness. Our conversations had become such an integral part of my life, and the idea of seeing him face-to-face was both thrilling and daunting. But as much as I looked forward to that moment, it was overshadowed by the overwhelming pull of family.

The love and connection I felt for my parents, my siblings, and even the memories of my childhood were stronger, more immediate. They were the reason I had come back, and they were what mattered most. Shannu was important, yes, but he was a part of a different world—a world I couldn't let myself fully step into. For now, my heart belonged to the family waiting for me, and that was where I needed to be.

We landed in the early hours of the morning, the airport bustling with activity. The kids were tired but excited, their eyes wide as they took in the new surroundings. Rohan handled the luggage while I kept an eye on the kids, making sure they didn't wander off.

As we made our way through the airport, I couldn't help but glance around, half-expecting to see Shannu waiting for us. But he wasn't there. He had told me he wouldn't come to the airport, that he wanted to give us space to settle in first. I understood, but a part of me wished he was there.

We were greeted by my sister and her family at the arrival gate, their faces lighting up at the sight of us greeting them personally. There were hugs and tears, and for a moment, I forgot about everything else.

Shannu had been counting down the days, each one bringing him closer to the moment he would finally meet his Ammu in person. He had imagined this moment countless times, but now that it was here, he felt a mix of excitement and nervousness.

He had decided not to go to the airport, wanting to give her space to reunite with her family. But as the hours ticked by, he found it hard to focus on anything else. His mind kept drifting to thoughts of her—her smile, her laughter, the way her eyes lit up when she talked about something she was passionate about.

He had prepared for this meeting meticulously, choosing a quiet restaurant where they could talk without distractions. He wanted everything to be perfect, but more than that, he wanted her to feel comfortable.

As he waited, his thoughts turned to their conversations over the past months. They had shared so much—their dreams, their fears, their pasts. He had come to care for her deeply, more than he had ever expected. But he also knew the boundaries they had to respect.

The wait is over

Waiting is a silent symphony, composed in the hollows of the heart where hope and fear waltz in endless circles. It is the breath held between moments, the unspoken hymn of longing that hums beneath the skin. For Shannu, waiting was not a passive act but a pilgrimage—a journey through time where every tick of the clock echoed like a footstep drawing nearer. He sat in the quiet café, fingers tracing the rim of his untouched coffee cup, as if the ceramic curve could anchor him to the present. Outside, the Hyderabad sun blazed, but within him, shadows stretched, slow and patient, like vines creeping toward light.

The air thickened with the scent of cardamom and simmering chai, but Shannu tasted only the metallic tang of anticipation. His mind wandered to the airport, where Ammu's plane had kissed the tarmac hours ago. He imagined her stepping into the humid embrace of their homeland, her children's hands clasped in hers, her husband's presence a steady shadow beside her. He wondered if her eyes still carried that quiet storm he'd glimpsed in pixels and pixels of late-night chats. Waiting, he realized, was not emptiness—it was a vessel overflowing with ghosts of *what-ifs* and *maybes*, each one lapping at the edges of his resolve.

Time bent like a blade of grass beneath the weight of his thoughts. The café's ceiling fan whirred, slicing the stillness into fragments. He rehearsed sentences that dissolved like sugar in tea, words too sweet or too bitter to hold their shape. Would she recognize the man he'd become—the writer who'd spun sonnets from their shared silences? Or would she see only the boy who once loved her from afar, his heart a flickering lamp in the dark? Waiting, he learned, was a mirror. It showed him not just the man he was, but the man he might have been, had life's threads woven a different pattern.

And then, the door chimed. The world sharpened—the clatter of plates, the murmur of strangers, the sudden intake of breath.

There she stood, framed by sunlight, her laughter a melody he'd forgotten he knew by heart. In that moment, waiting collapsed into a single, crystalline truth: it was never about the end, but the ache of becoming. The space between them—a breath, a heartbeat, a lifetime—was both bridge and abyss. And Shannu, poet of the unspoken, understood this: to wait is to love in past tense, to cradle a flame that burns brighter for every second it goes untouched.

As he waited, he rehearsed what he would say, how he would act. He wanted to be warm, friendly, but not too familiar. He wanted to show her how much she meant to him, but without crossing the line. It was a delicate balance; one he wasn't sure he could maintain.

When the time finally came, and he saw her walking towards him, his heart skipped a beat.

The sound of the door opening snapped him out of his thoughts. He looked up, and there she was—Manjula, more beautiful in person than he had ever imagined. She was even more beautiful in person, her presence filling the room with a warmth that made him feel at home. She was followed by Rohan, a tall, composed man who exuded a quiet confidence, and their two children, who looked around the restaurant with wide-eyed curiosity.

Shannu stood up, his heart pounding as he greeted them. "Manjula, it's so good to finally meet you," he said, his voice steady despite the storm of emotions inside him.

Manjula smiled, her eyes lighting up in a way that made his heart ache. "Shannu, it's wonderful to see you. This is my husband, Rohan, and our children, Taara and Vihaan."

Shannu shook Rohan's hand, his grip firm but not overbearing. "It's a pleasure to meet you," he said, his tone polite but warm.

As they sat down to lunch, Shannu couldn't help but feel a pang of sadness. Manjula was everything he had imagined and more, but she was also someone else's wife, someone else's mother. He knew he had to tread carefully, to keep his emotions in check.

The conversation flowed easily, filled with laughter and stories. Shannu found himself drawn to Taara and Vihaan, their innocence and curiosity a refreshing change from the complexities of adult life. He made them laugh with silly jokes and stories, earning their instant approval.

But it was Manjula who held his attention, her presence a constant reminder of the connection they shared. He caught her eye occasionally, and in those moments, he felt a spark of something unspoken, something that neither of them could—or would—acknowledge.

As the lunch came to an end, Shannu felt a mix of relief and sadness. He had managed to keep his emotions in check, to maintain the boundaries that separated them. But he also knew that this meeting had only deepened his feelings for her, making it even harder to keep them hidden.

As they said their goodbyes, Shannu hugged Manjula, a brief, fleeting moment of connection that left him breathless. "Take care, Ammu," he whispered, his voice barely audible.

Manjula nodded; her eyes filled with a mixture of emotions. "You too, Shannu."

As he watched them walk away, Shannu felt a sense of closure, but also a lingering ache. He had met the woman he loved, but she was not his to keep. And in that moment, he knew that he would carry her in his heart, always.

The Unwritten Epilogue

Time, that quiet thief, had a way of softening edges. Months folded into years, and the ache of unsent words between Manjula and Shannu settled into a dull hum, like a forgotten melody played on a distant radio. Shannu returned to his world of ink and paper, his stories now tinged with a bittersweet hue. He wrote of love that lingered in the margins, of characters who loved fiercely but chose duty over desire. His readers called it his most profound work; only he knew it was a eulogy.

In India, Manjula's days were a tapestry of routine—school runs, grocery lists, her husband's steady presence. But sometimes, in the lull of afternoon silence or the glow of a monsoon dusk, she'd catch herself reaching for her phone, thumb hovering over Shannu's name. Memories would surge: his laughter during their video calls, the way he'd called her Ammu like it was a secret only they shared. She'd close her eyes, breathe deep, and let the moment pass. To text him would be to unearth a ghost, and she feared what might follow—his voice cracking with longing, or worse, the silence of a reply never sent.

One evening, her younger sister, visited, her curiosity piqued by Manjula's quiet transformation. Over chai,

Priya asked, *"Does marriage change everyone, or is it just you?"*

Manjula stirred her tea, watching sugar crystals dissolve.

"It's like becoming a river," she said.

"You carve new paths, but the old currents never leave. You're both the flow and the stone it wears down."

Priya blinked, perplexed. *"That's... deep. But are you **happy**?"*

Manjula smiled, a fragile thing. *"Happiness is a tide. It comes and goes. What stays is the shore you build."*

ುುು

Later, alone on the terrace, Manjula gazed at the stars, their light a cold comfort. She thought of Shannu—how he'd once compared her to a constellation, beautiful and just out of reach. The night breeze carried the scent of jasmine, and for a heartbeat, she let herself imagine typing a message: *Do you still write about us?*

But she didn't.

Instead, she whispered to the dark, her voice swallowed by the wind: A thought to herself.

"He'll be remembered in many ways and the most hardest truth is I always keep him close to my heart. I will never forget that he calls me his Ammu."

ᐅᐅᐅ

omewhere, in another city, Shannu paused mid-sentence, his pen trembling. The words felt like an echo, a shard of a dream he'd almost forgotten. He smiled, faint and sorrowful, and wrote:

To Ammu—whose colours still bleed into my blank pages.

ᐅᐅᐅ

And so, they remained: *two stories*, bound by a chapter they dared not write.

2
Between two heartbeats

Love has its own rhythm—sometimes it flows in harmony, and sometimes it collides with fate in the most unexpected ways.

Love doesn't always follow the rules we set for it.

It blooms in unexpected places, crosses forbidden boundaries, and sometimes, it leaves behind unfinished stories.

Some love stories don't end in togetherness, but that doesn't mean they are incomplete.

This is a story of love in its purest form—one that teaches, transforms, and finds its own way, even in separation.

Love, when true, is never selfish.

The Unseen Threads

The Yamuna lay sluggish under a veil of factory smog, its banks choked with skeletal frames of half-built and abandoned homes. Delhi in '93 was a beast gnawing at the bones of liberalization—its streets a chaotic symphony of Ambassador horns, cycle-rickshaws, and the occasional Maruti 800 sputtering past faded "India Shining" posters.

Sagar's government quarter in Patel Nagar smelled of damp cement and kerosene, the walls thin enough to hear his neighbor's transistor blaring *Chitralahari* updates. Even in Delhi, someone played Telugu songs every day. He had arrived two years ago, a transfer clerk from the Panchayat office in Visakhapatnam to the Urban Development Ministry, carrying little more than a steel trunk, a threadbare kurta, worn-out copies of Sri Sri, and two chains made of gold and silver tucked in a velvet pouch.

His desk at the ministry faced a grime-streaked window overlooking Okhla's industrial sprawl. By day, he processed permits for textile mills and cement factories, his fingers stained with carbon paper ink. But it was the evenings that defined him—the supplicants who found their way to his doorstep. Villagers from Haryana, their *gamchas* dust-laden from bus rides, clutching land deeds in trembling hands. Widows fumbling with pension forms, eyes searching for help.

"Saab, yeh stamp kahan lagana hai?" they'd ask, and Sagar, his voice steady as chai poured in slow circles, would reply, *"Yahan, chacha. Darr mat."*

One monsoon evening, a farmer from Rewari collapsed outside his office, his son's polio treatment denied by a clerk demanding a bribe. Sagar carried the man to a bench, offered him black tea, and spent the night rewriting the application in flawless Hindi. By dawn, the stamp was secured—no palms greased, no favours called. The farmer wept, pressing a fistful of barley into Sagar's hands. He refused the gift but kept a single grain in his pocket, a silent talisman against the creeping cynicism around him.

The letter arrived on a Tuesday, its envelope the pale blue of a school uniform. Sagar recognized the handwriting instantly—looping, confident, the *m* in 'Anniversary' curling like a smirk. Inside, a card adorned with lotus motifs:

ᏇᏇᏇ

Dear Sagar,

First year. Can't believe it. I never imagined you would break your promise, but when you didn't show up at my wedding, I realized some bonds aren't as strong as I believed. But you'd definitely taste my strong punch breaking your bones when you come to my anniversary party—and that's a promise, my dear friend.

Come to Bangalore. 15th *July. No excuses this time.*

*– **Chandram***

ᏇᏇᏇ

He hadn't gone to the wedding. That day, a year ago, he'd sat on the Visakhapatnam railway platform, ticket crumpled in his fist, until the train whistled away. The velvet pouch around his neck had never felt heavier.

Now, he traced the gold border of the card, memories rising like heatwaves.

Summer, '79. Chandram, just ten, running alongside Sagar, fingers tight on the handlebars of a wobbly bicycle. The dirt path behind their Kendriya Vidyalaya stretched uneven and unforgiving.

"Pedal, yaar! Eyes ahead!" Chandram's voice rang with laughter, firm and insistent.

Sagar's legs trembled, his grip unsteady, but he pushed forward, trusting the hands that held him upright. Then, a sudden swerve—his knee scraped against the gravel, dust clinging to fresh blood. He winced, bracing for scolding, but Chandram only grinned.

"Again," he said, offering a hand.

Winter afternoons beneath the old neem tree, sunlight dappling the schoolyard. Chandram unwrapping his tiffin, wrinkling his nose at semya upma before swapping it for Sagar's pulihora.

"Your mother cooks like a saint. Mine's trying to kill me," he grumbled, shoveling food into his mouth.

Sagar had only laughed. Tomorrow, they'd trade again—different meals, same words, the quiet language of friendship spoken through stainless steel lunchboxes.

ꢾꢾꢾ

He found the perfect gift at Ganguly Brothers, where the air carried the scent of aging paper and polished wood. A timepiece—elegant, precise. Chandram had always believed gifts should have meaning, not just function.

"A wall clock," he used to say, *"isn't just to mark hours. It's a reminder of love that lingers, even when time moves on."*

At the counter, an old Sikh shopkeeper tied the twine around the package, his gaze curious.

"For a friend?"

"For a brother," Sagar replied, the gold chain cool against his chest.

The Karnataka Express pulled away from New Delhi Station at 7:15 PM. Sleeper Coach S3, berth 27. The compartment hummed with the familiar rhythms of an Indian train—mothers bundling children under shawls, college students debating Mandal Commission protests, a Gujarati businessman snoring into his *Saraswatichandra* paperback.

Near Bhopal, a delay—a goods train derailment. Vendors lined the platform, selling *samosas* wrapped in old newspapers, their voices merging with the heat. Sagar remained seated, fingers brushing the spine of *Mahaprasthanam,* his reflection fractured in the windowpane.

Somewhere near Nagpur, sleep pulled him under. He dreamt of a girl dancing in the monsoon rain, her anklets ringing like temple bells.

At dawn, Bangalore unfolded before him—air crisp with eucalyptus and diesel. Auto-rickshaws swarmed like yellow beetles, drivers shouting, *"MG Road! Frazer Town!"* The breeze carried something familiar—jasmine? Sandalwood?

For a heartbeat, his chest tightened.

The city reminded him of something.

Adjusting his spectacles, he stepped forward, the gold chain pulsing under his shirt, a secret even the wind couldn't steal.

Its her

Sagar took a cab to *Leela Kempinski*, bargaining fiercely with the driver before settling into the rear seat. He let out a deep breath, his suitcase safely stowed in the trunk, and watched the city blur past in streaks of neon and monsoon-damp streets.

The *Leela Kempinski* rose like a cream-colored fortress on Old Airport Road, its Rajputana arches and Mughal *jaalis* glowing under halogen lamps. His ambassador rattled to a halt beneath the portico, tires crunching over gravel still wet from an evening drizzle. A doorman in a gold-braided sherwani swung the door open, unleashing a wave of air tinged with tuberose and sandalwood. The lobby stretched vast before him—marble floors gleaming under a peacock-shaped crystal chandelier, its prismed light dancing with the distant clink of champagne glasses.

Sagar paid the driver exact change— ₹75, no tip—and hoisted his satchel over his shoulder, its leather worn from Delhi's monsoons. The receptionist, her bindi a perfect crimson dot, handed him a brass key labelled 217. The elevator's mirrored doors closed with a shudder, trapping his reflection—a man caught between past and present.

The room was a time capsule of 90s opulence: teakwood furniture, a rotary phone resting on a lace doily, a Philips television crackling with static. He unlatched his suitcase, unfolding a mauve silk kurta—Benarasi, bought from Palika Bazaar for ₹1,200, a month's salary. The shower drizzled lukewarm water, lemongrass-scented soap scrubbing away the last traces of coal dust from his train journey. The kurta clung to his shoulders, its embroidery catching the light like veins of silver.

The banquet hall thrummed with a Hindi film orchestra's rendition of "*Pehla Nasha.*" Saxophone notes slithered between buffet tables stacked with tandoori prawns and rasmalai. Chandram stood by the bar, his navy blazer cutting a sharp silhouette against the gold-lit crowd. He turned just as Sagar approached, his grin widening into a roar.

"*Saala! Two years, and you show up now?*" Chandram's punch landed soft against Sagar's ribs—a brotherly jab. His cologne, Jovan Musk, rushed over Sagar in a wave of familiarity.

"*I'm sorry, yaar. That transfer to Delhi...*" Sagar's voice wavered.

"*Transfer? You vanished like a chor after my wedding! Ma kept asking, 'Did we offend him?'*" Chandram laughed, but his eyes narrowed—ever the observer.

Sagar handed over his gift. "*May this always remind you that every moment spent together is a timeless treasure, growing more precious with each passing year. Happy Anniversary!*"

Chandram's brows lifted in astonishment. "*Since when did you become a poet?!*"

"*Since you lectured me on how to buy a meaningful gift!*"

Laughter erupted around them, warmth spilling into the space between old friends. Then, with a sudden solemnity, Chandram clasped Sagar's hand, his voice thick with emotion.

"*Thanks for coming, ra. I missed you. Come, let me introduce you to my wife.*"

She stood by the grand piano, back turned, peacock-blue Kanjeevaram silk pooling at her feet. The hall's chandeliers bathed her chignon in golden light, a single jasmine strand woven into the knot. Chandram touched her elbow.

"*Sandhya, this is Sagar. My oldest friend.*"

She turned.

Time cracked.

Her eyes—those eyes—widened, but she gave nothing away. Not to Chandram. Not to the world. But in that moment, the air thickened with the salt-scent of RK Beach, the memory of a gold chain clutched in a downpour, a thousand unsent letters. A million memories rushed at her, clawing for release, but she held them back, locking them behind an unreadable gaze.

"*A pleasure,*" she said, her voice steady yet fragile. Her hand hovered in the space between them, a gold bangle glinting under the chandelier's glow—an invitation and a warning all at once.

Sagar grasped it, the warmth of her skin searing into his palm. *"The honour is mine... Mrs. Chandram."*

Chandram clapped his shoulder. *"Sandhya's a dancer—Mayuri, they call her! You'd love her performances."*

You should have met her long back, during the wedding. But you lost the moment.

Sagar's spectacles fogged. *"Yes. I've... heard about her reputation. And it's true—I lost the moment... forever."*

Across the hall, a clock chimed. Sandhya bowed; hands pressed together in a namaste. Her deep blue sari shimmered like a peacock spreading its tail, woven with threads of green and gold. But unlike a peacock, free in its dance, her movements were measured, precise. The tiny bells that once jingled at her ankles were now muffled beneath silk, their silence a cruel twist of fate.

Sagar watched her vanish into the crowd, his gift's ticking clock pounding in his ears.

Speak—your lips are free.

But the gold chain around his neck strangled every word.

꧁꧂꧂

The Bangalore night hung thick with jacaranda musk, their purple petals carpeting the driveway of Chandram's bungalow. Sandhya lay rigid under the mosquito net, the gauze a ghostly veil in the dim light. The ceiling fan whirred; its rhythm syncopated with Chandram's deep, untroubled snores—each breath an unbearable reminder of her own unease.

The echoes of the evening clawed at her—Sagar's trembling fingers, the fog on his glasses, the unspoken weight between them. He was here. In Bangalore. Alive.

Quietly, she slipped out of bed. The garden below was a tapestry of shadows—neem branches clawing at the moon, bougainvillea spilling over the compound wall like dried blood. Somewhere, a stray dog howled, its cry slicing through the hush of sleeping streets.

She touched her throat.

The chain was still there—the one she'd sworn never to remove. Its cold links burned against her skin. Slowly, deliberately, she yanked it free, letting the silver pool in her palm like liquid moonlight. A wild thought seized her—hurl it into the gulmohar tree, let the night swallow it whole.

But her fingers tightened. The locket's edges pressed into her skin, marking her.

Some memories could not be discarded.

Some chains could never be broken.

Monsoon Stories

The sky hung low over Bangalore, a quilt of leaden clouds threatening to burst. Chandram's bungalow in Indiranagar lay quiet, save for the rhythmic tick-tock of the cuckoo clock—a gift from Sagar. Sandhya sat by the teakwood window, her fingers absently tracing the grooves of the silver chain beneath her saree's pallu. The monsoon had left the garden sodden—hibiscus blooms drooping like defeated flags, the guava tree's branches sagging under the weight of unripe fruit.

A knock. Three precise raps.

She knew it was him before she opened the door.

Sagar stood on the veranda, his umbrella dripping onto the cracked mosaic tiles. He wore a cream-colored kurta, its collar slightly frayed, and held a packet of apples—Chandram's favourite. His spectacles were fogged, but not enough to hide the flicker in his eyes when he saw her. She looked the same. A year of marriage hadn't changed her much. Her steps still carried the grace of a dancer. She was the same *Mayuri* he once admired.

"He's… not home," Sandhya said, stepping aside. Her voice was steady, polished by years of stagecraft. Her eyes held his, unwavering.

Sagar lingered for a moment, taking her in. Then, softly, he said, *"I'll wait."*

He settled on the edge of the cane sofa, back rigid, while she busied herself in the kitchen. The smell of filter coffee bloomed—Chandram's preference, strong and black. She poured two cups anyway, the steel tumblers clinking as she carried them in.

Rain drummed the asbestos roof. He remembered a peacock dancing for rain.

"You look happy," Sagar said, cradling his cup. The red thread on his wrist peeked from his sleeve, frayed but stubbornly intact. He looked at her over the rim of his cup. She had a smile on her lips—the kind that held poems. Poems only he could decipher.

"So do you."

A lie. Delhi had etched shadows under his eyes, sharpened his cheekbones. He always seemed to lead a forceful life there, waiting for something he'd lost. His eyes spoke a million stories to the one who could read them. She wondered if he noticed the way her mangalsutra dug into her neck, a golden shackle. She didn't know why, but she was happy looking at him.

The silence stretched, taut as a veena string. Somewhere, a bicycle bell jingled, muffled by the downpour.

"Chandram—" they began together, then stopped.

Sandhya gestured for him to continue.

"He's a good man," Sagar said, staring into his coffee. *"He deserves happiness."*

"He is." Her thumb brushed the locket of her chain, its edges biting her skin. *"He doesn't know. About... us."*

"I know."

Sagar wanted to say more, but the words dissolved on his tongue. Sandhya waited, giving him space. Maybe some things were best left buried. He smiled at her instead. A quiet, bittersweet smile.

With wet eyes, she returned it.

The air grew heavier with unspoken words.

A crack of thunder rattled the windowpanes. Sagar's cup trembled, pulling him back from a thought. A dark droplet stained his kurta. Sandhya reached for a napkin, her hand grazing his. Time stuttered.

For a heartbeat, the room dissolved—Vizag's sunlit beaches replaced Bangalore's gloom, the coffee's bitterness swapped with the tang of sea salt on lips.

Then she withdrew, the moment buried under the cuckoo clock's mocking chirp.

Sagar stood abruptly. *"I should go."*

At the door, he hesitated. He looked back, stealing one more second of her presence. *"Be happy, Sandhya. Truly."*

She nodded, the chain searing her collarbone. *"You too, Sagar."*

When the gate creaked shut, she slid to the floor, her saree pooling like a fallen peacock's plume. Outside, the rain wept.

The next day, Sagar left for Delhi. He phoned Chandram to say goodbye. Nothing more. Just a short *'bye.'*

ᐅᐅᐅ

Chandram's love was not a wildfire, but a slow monsoon—steady, drenching, seeping into the cracks of Sandhya's parched heart. In the early days, his kindness felt like a borrowed sari, beautiful but ill-fitting. He'd leave Ravindra Kale poetry books on her pillow, their margins scribbled with Telugu translations. He memorized her coffee ritual—one spoon sugar, a pinch of cardamom—and brewed it himself before dawn.

On Sundays, he drove her to Nrityagram, the dance academy on Bangalore's outskirts, though he loathed the traffic on Hosur Road. He'd wait in the car, Deccan Herald in hand, while she taught Kathak to wide-eyed girls. "Your eyes light up here," he remarked once, tapping the rearview mirror as they left. *"Like diyas on Diwali."*

Their home became a museum of small surrenders:

- His leather briefcase parked beside her dance anklets in the entryway.
- Her Kumkum smudges on his white office shirts, laundered but never fully erased.
- The nights he feigned sleep just to hear her hum M.S. Subbulakshmi under her breath, her voice an addiction to his boardroom-weary mind.

When monsoons lashed the city, Chandram would drag the sofa to the veranda, wordlessly handing her a bowl of sakkarai pongal as they watched rain sluice off the mango trees. No grand gestures—just his thumb brushing hers when she reached for more jaggery.

Yet, the truest measure of her happiness lay in the absences:

- The dwindling nights she woke clutching the chain around her neck.
- The way Chandram's laugh—a deep, rumbling thing, like a train crossing a bridge—began to anchor her dreams instead of Sagar's whispers.
- The morning she forgot to knot her pallu over the chain, letting it rest openly beside her mangalsutra, two talismans of two loves—one buried, one breathing.

She never called it passion. But in the quiet alchemy of shared silences and half-smiles, Sandhya learned to stitch a new life from the remnants of the old, thread by thread, until the fabric held.

That night, Sandhya opened her photo album—her best-kept secret for two years. She turned the pages, memories unfurling like the scent of old paper. Some made her lips curve in a quiet smile; others pulled a drop from her eyes.

She missed a lot of things. Her friends. Her tea parties. Bicycle races. Movies.

And *Sagar.*

Sandya's Sagar

The air in Visakhapatnam's Rama Krishna Beach Auditorium hung thick with the scent of jasmine and anticipation. Backstage, Sandhya adjusted her *arakku*—the crimson border of her silk saree—her fingers trembling imperceptibly. The anklet bells, a cascade of silver ghungroos, chimed softly as she stepped into the spotlight. The audience hushed. A single mridangam beat thudded, and she became *Mayuri*—the peacock.

Her arangetram was no mere debut; it was an invocation. Each *adavu* was precision—hips swivelling like temple carvings come alive, eyes darting with the sharpness of a bird's gaze, her mudras weaving tales of Radha's longing and Durga's fury. When she spun, the zari on her davani caught the light, scattering gold flecks across the front row where her parents sat. Her mother's pallu was already damp with tears; her father, a retired schoolmaster, clutched his dhoti pleats, pride tautening his jaw.

By morning, she was Sandhya again—a student, a daughter, a friend. At Andhra University's MA Literature department, her Kumkum-stained notebooks brimmed with annotations of *Tagore* and *Nannaya*. She excelled in studies, dance, event organization, and managing emotions with grace. "*Miss Rao*," Professor Iyer would say, adjusting his wire-framed glasses, "*your essay on Silappadikaram's feminist undertones—brilliant. Have you considered doctoral studies?*"

She'd smile, the same serene curve she reserved for admirers who lingered after lectures. "*Dance is my first language, sir. Literature... its echo.*"

Her classmates oscillated between awe and envy. Priya, her roommate, once failed a paper on Bharatanatyam's socio-cultural impact, and Sandhya spent nights dissecting Abhinaya Darpana with her, translating Sanskrit shlokas into Telugu over milky chai. "*You're too good*," Priya sighed, half-joking. "*Save some genius for the rest of us.*"

Sandhya laughed, a sound like temple bells. "*Genius is practice wearing a bindi, Priya.*" She believed in service to humanity as service to the divine. Help had often come to her in unseen ways, strengthening her faith.

Her flat in Dwarakanagar smelled perpetually of sambhar and sandalwood. Her mother, Lakshmi, ritualistically placed a *Vibhuti* dot on Sandhya's forehead each morning. "*The stage lights will steal your glow,*" she fretted, packing tiffin of lemon rice.

Her father, Surya, hid his pride behind The Hindu's editorials. "*This article on caste politics...*" he'd grumble, peering over his spectacles. "*You'll face such fools in life. Stay sharp.*" She'd nod, knowing his gruffness masked a father's fear of losing his brightest star to a world unkind to women who shone too boldly.

Admirers flocked like moths. Rajesh, the engineering student, penned awful haikus comparing her eyes to Bhimili's moonlit waves. Anil, a junior dancer, left gajra garlands at her doorstep. Even Professor Menon, stoic in his khadi kurta, once slipped a Kalidasa anthology into her bag with a note: "*For the muse who outshines her art.*"

She declined them all with grace. "*My heart's rhythm belongs to the taalam,*" she told Rajesh. To Anil: "*Offer your flowers to the sea—they'll reach a goddess.*"

Only her childhood friend, Meera, dared tease. "*You'll die a spinster, Mayuri.*"

Sandhya shrugged, braiding her hair with coconut oil. "*Better than being a caged peacock.*"

Yet, in the quiet hours between rehearsal and dawn, she dreamed of a love as intricate as a Bharatanatyam recital—someone whose soul would harmonize with hers in every *tala* and *laya*. A man who'd see beyond the Mayuri persona, who'd cherish the sweat-stained practice saris and ink-smudged poetry journals as fiercely as her stage glory. A partner who'd kneel beside her to fasten her ghungroos, not out of duty, but reverence; who'd debate Tagore over filter *kaapi*, his eyes alight with kinship, not mere infatuation.

Sagar first saw Sandhya perform at Visakhapatnam's Sri Venkateswara Kala Vedika in 1991, his clerk's salary barely affording the torn ticket stub. By the third jathi, he was no longer breathing—he was witnessing. When she became *Draupadi*, her eyes blazing as she mimed tearing off her sari in defiance, Sagar's pen slipped, ink bleeding across the panchayat ledger he'd brought to draft meeting minutes. That night, he wrote his first poem in a decade: *"Her feet etch rebellion / the stage weeps silver / and I, a moth, circle her flame."*

He attended every performance, never approaching her, content to leave a single *mogra* on her greenroom sill. When she danced, he memorized the cadence of her breath, the way her little finger quivered before a spin—details invisible to the roaring crowd.

At the university canteen, he lingered two tables away, pretending to read Sri Sri's *Mahaprasthanam* while she debated Amrita Pritam with classmates. Once, she dropped a kumkum-stained note on caste dynamics; he returned it anonymously, his margin notes in Telugu poetry: *"The river doesn't ask the stone's caste before embracing it."*

His gifts—a dog-eared Faiz anthology, a spool of *arakku* thread for her torn saree—spoke louder than Rajesh's haikus or Anil's garlands. He once left a palm-leaf fan backstage during a summer recital, its handle carved with a peacock feather. No name, just a scribble: *"For the sweat of the gods envy."*

When her father fell ill, Sagar queued for hours at the government hospital to secure a specialist referral, bribing no one, his clerk's badge granting no favours. He never told her.

His threadbare shirts hid a silver chain—his late mother's, a Dalit woman who'd scrubbed floors to send him to school. He understood caste's cruel calculus but wore his scars softly, his voice a calm river hiding undercurrents of rage and resolve.

Sagar loved like a *thillana*—complex, layered, his silence a counterpoint to her crescendos. He didn't seek to "complete" her; he was the *taalam* to her *ragam*, grounding her flight without clipping her wings. In another life, unshackled from duty and division, he'd have been the man who fastened her ghungroos each dawn.

But in this life, he was the admirer who gifted a peacock-feather fan, the clerk who wept in the back row, the poet who never signed his verses.

The Kala Bharati Auditorium exhaled its last applause, the crowd funnelling into the muggy Visakhapatnam night. Backstage, Sandhya dabbed her neck with a damp towel, the kumkum from her bindi smudging into a teardrop. A knock—hesitant, rhythmic—tapped the door.

"Come."

Sagar stood framed in the doorway, a wilted tuberose in one hand and a notebook in the other. His white kurta clung to his collarbones, damp from the cycle ride, and his spectacles trembled as if the ground beneath him had slipped.

"S..an.dhya…" he faltered, his Telugu stumbling. *"Your Padam tonight… the way you held the simhanandana pose—like Devi balancing the cosmos. I… I wrote something."*

He thrust the notebook forward. She took it, her fingers grazing the paper, still warm from his grip. The verses were raw, unpolished—just truth.

In the amber spill of stage light,
your shadow unfurls—a silent peacock
fanning obsidian plumes.
I count the beats: ta-ka-dhimi-ta,
your ghungroos etching time
into the fissures of this borrowed world.
*   You spin, and the dark twin follows—*
a lover's echo, a debt unpaid.
Seventeen times, the earth forgets its axis.
Seventeen times, I forget my name.
*   They see only the gold—*
the sweat-slick glow, the mudras
that sculpt gods from air.
I trace the edges they ignore—
the frayed hem of your defiance,
the whisper of hesitation
before your wrist bends to the sky
we were never meant to claim.
*   Your shadow drinks the light I lack,*
bold where I shrink.
At night, it slips between ledgers,
filling margins with unscripted jathis—
footprints of a dance
that could have been ours.
*   When dawn smears its vermilion across my window,*
I find it curled on the floor,
a question without language:
*   What is a shadow, if not love's stubborn ghost?*
A silhouette untethered, aching, endless,
in the cruel grammar of light.
*   And so I write us down—*
not in ink, nor in rhythm,
but in the silence between two heartbeats.

"*You've seen my shows before,*" she said, not a question.

"Twenty-seven." His voice steadied. "*Since the arangetram. I sit in the last row. The lights hit your odhni there—it looks like a phoenix wing.*"

A moth batted against the lone bulb overhead. Sandhya gestured to the stool beside her makeup mirror. "*Sit.*"

He perched on the edge, spine straight, as if braced for judgment. She noticed his shoes—scuffed Bata sandals, the left strap repaired with bicycle tape.

"*Why today?*"

He removed his spectacles, polishing them on his sleeve. "*Your abhinaya during the viraha sequence—it wasn't longing. It was rage.*"

She stilled. No critic, no guru, had ever named that secret.

"*You changed the mudra here.*" He mimicked her gesture—a twisted katakamukha instead of the traditional pataka. "*Like Draupadi clutching her sari, not pleading.*"

The room tilted. Sandhya's pulse thrummed in her ghungroo-bruised ankles. Here was a man who had dissected her art down to the tremor of a finger.

"*Why a clerk?*" she whispered. "*You should be... a poet. A scholar.*"

His laugh was a soft, broken thing. "*Poetry doesn't feed my family.*"

They talked as the night deepened—of Sri Sri's rebellion, Amrita Pritam's silenced verses, the hypocrisy of saints who preached equality but wedlocked their daughters to caste. His words were calloused hands offering her shattered glass, each shard a mirror to her own stifled rebellions.

When he rose to leave, she gripped his wrist. "*Your poem... the line about the 'silence'—what did you mean?*"

Sagar's thumb brushed her alta-stained toe, a touch so light it could have been the breeze. "*That some stories don't need endings. They're alive as long as... someone remembers.*"

Outside, the Bay of Bengal roared. Sagar presented Sandhya with his mother's silver chain—it had a twin to complete it and he shared one with her—warmed against her skin. He left with a namaste.

That night, Sandhya didn't fall in love with a man. She fell for the shadow who had memorized her light.

ᐯᐯᐯ

Sandhya first sensed Sagar's depth not through words, but through the silence he wore like a second skin. It was in the way he lingered after her performances, never jostling for praise like others, but standing apart—a silhouette against the auditorium's exit, his spectacles catching the stage's dying light. One evening, she found a spool of *arakku* thread tied to her greenroom mirror, the exact shade of her torn practice saree. No note, just a peacock feather tucked beneath it. That's when she knew: his love was a language of gaps and gestures, a poem written in the margins of the ordinary.

At Andhra University's canteen, amidst the clatter of steel plates and the tang of tamarind rice, their conversations unfolded in stolen glances and half-smiles. Sagar always chose the corner table, its vinyl peeling like sunburned skin, a copy of Faiz shielding his face. Sandhya, flanked by giggling classmates, would *"forget"* her kumkum-stained notes beside his chair. He'd return them with verses scribbled in the margins:

"Why does the cuckoo sing only in spring? Doesn't it know the monsoon hears it best?"

Once, during a power cut, their hands brushed reaching for the same glass of mosambi juice. The room buzzed back to life, but they remained suspended in that dark, accidental touch—a spark that outshone the flickering tube lights.

RK Beach became their cathedral. During evenings, Sandhya would shed her *Mayuri*, swapping silk for a cotton *pavadai*, her hair loose and salt-kissed. Sagar arrived on his rusted cycle, for her. For his *Mayuri*.

They walked where the waves erased footprints, speaking in riddles and truths:

Sandhya: *"Why do you hide behind poetry?"*

Sagar: *"For the same reason you dance—to survive what can't be said."*

He once knelt to tie her pallu when the wind lashed it free, his fingers lingering at her waist. She didn't pull away. The lighthouse at Dolphin's Nose blinked twice, as if sealing their secret.

Backstage, he became her silent ally. While others praised her grace, he noticed the blisters on her toes, slipping a tin of Margo neem oil into her bag. During a *varnam* rehearsal, she faltered, her ankle buckling mid-spin. The gurus scowled; Sagar, sweeping the wings, hummed a raga under his breath—*Kalyani*, her favourite—steadying her rhythm.

One monsoon night, stranded by a heavy rain, they huddled under the auditorium's awning. Sandhya, shivering in the cold, felt his kurta drape her shoulders—still warm from his skin. He recited a verse:

"Your art is a storm. I am the earth that learns to thirst for it."

She laughed, breath fogging the air between them. *"You're terrible at metaphors."*

"But you're smiling," he said. And she was.

𐤘𐤘𐤘

The ceiling fan wobbled overhead, its blades chopping the silence into jagged fragments. Sandhya's father stood framed by the kitchen doorway, his veshti crisply pleated, eyes avoiding hers. *"Kanna, we've finalized your match. A Bangalore boy—senior manager, Brahmin, earns well. His family values culture."*

Sandhya's kumkum trembled on her forehead. *"Appa, I'm only twen—"*

"Enough." His palm smacked the table, rattling the steel tumbler. *"You think dancers stay stars forever? This is security. Our security."*

That night, she found Sagar at their rock—the one shaped like a crouching lion, salt-scarred and stubborn. His bicycle leaned against the stone, its handlebars rusted, a wilted mograw in the basket.

"I'm getting married," she said.

A wave exploded against the rocks. Sagar's spectacles fogged.

She waited for anger, for pleas. Instead, he smiled—a fractured thing. *"Bangalore's... nice. Good weather."*

His calm snapped her. She lunged into him, fists clenching his kurta, sobs erupting like blood from a wound. *"Take me away. Please. Anywhere."*

He held her, his silence a language they'd mastered. His fingers traced the chain around her neck, the one he had given her months ago, his mother's final heirloom.

"You keep it," he had insisted then. *"She'd want you to have it."*

Now, it felt like a noose.

After a month, the Vizag station swallowed Sagar whole—a clerk's trunk, a third-class ticket, and a transfer letter crumpled in his fist. He didn't glance back. He left. Not with a farewell, but with the quiet finality of a man erasing his shadow.

On the same day, she was getting married. Sandhya clasped the gold mangalsutra, its cold links a stranger's claim. As the *nadaswaram* wailed, she touched the silver chain hidden beneath, its edges dulled by salt and time. Somewhere, a peacock screamed.

ᐅᐅᐅ

The shores of Vizag had cradled their love in whispers—the kind that curled like incense smoke, fragile yet lingering. Sagar and Sandhya's romance had never roared; it flickered in stolen glances at Kalabharati Auditorium, in verses slipped between library books, in the brush of fingers over shared mosambi juice in the university canteen. Theirs was a love lit by the meek glow of a diya, its flame trembling but tenacious, casting shadows that swayed to a rhythm only they understood.

The night Sagar first spoke his love, they stood on RK Beach, the moon a smudged fingerprint on the sky. He came with no flowers, no grand declarations—only a palm-leaf scroll inscribed with a poem. "Your dance is not movement," he read, his voice quivering like the tide. "It is the pause between heartbeats." Sandhya had laughed, not in mockery but in wonder, her ghungroos jingling as she spun in the surf. In return, she unfastened her gold chain (gifted by her father), pressing it into his palm, its links still warm from her skin. "A trade," she teased.

"Your words for my silence."

For months, they met where the city's gaze could not follow—beneath the skeletal ribs of the Dolphin's Nose Lighthouse, in the dusty alcove of the Scindia Shipyard, even once within the hollow belly of the rusting INS Kursura submarine. Sagar's hands, calloused from filing panchayat records, mapped the geography of her blistered feet. Sandhya, whose voice commanded auditoriums, whispered secrets only he could hear—her fear of fading, the way her father's ambition curled around her like a golden cage. They spoke of impossible tomorrows: a tiny flat in Madras where she'd teach dance and he'd write; a coastal village where caste surnames would dissolve like salt in the sea.

But monsoons came.

The storm did not arrive with thunder, only with her father's clipped decree. "Chandram. Bangalore. Brahmin." Three words, and the diya's flame guttered.

Sandhya stood frozen in the family's prayer room, the air thick with camphor and crushed marigolds, her anklets still dusted with yesterday's rebellion.

The Return

Delhi had been a crucible of grit and bureaucracy—a city where ambition curdled under smog-streaked skies, where sunlight slithered through soot like a fugitive, leaving jaundiced stains on the walls of Sagar's cubicle. The air was thick with diesel and damp resignation, clogging his lungs as he shuffled stacks of paper stamped *URGENT* in blood-red ink—documents as forgotten as last year's monsoon.

His promotion letter arrived unceremoniously, sandwiched between a water bill and a Kwality Ice Cream coupon. The crisp Kannada script glared against the sea of Hindi paperwork:

"ಶ್ರೀಸಾಗರ್‌ರಾವ್, ಉಪಗುಮಾಸ್ತರು, ಕರ್ನಾಟಕಗ್ರಾಮೀಣಅಭಿವೃದ್ಧಿಮಂಡಳಿ. ತ್ವರಿತವರ್ಗಾವಣೆ: ಬೆಂಗಳೂರು."

Deputy Clerk. A title that was both a lifeline and a joke—a promise of escape, yet a reminder of fate's caprice.

He packed his life into a steel trunk that smelled of talcum powder and old ledgers, their spines cracked like tired bones, margins scribbled with forgotten Telugu couplets. Nestled inside: a peacock-feather quill plucked from Vizag's lighthouse rocks, its iridescence dulled by Delhi's dust. A silver chain, coiled in a velvet pouch that once cradled his mother's *mangalsutra*, leaving behind a faint, ghostly imprint—a serpentine scar of memory. A gold chain that always hangs around his neck.

The Karnataka Express thundered southward, its compartments thick with the musk of sweat and sambar. Sagar pressed his forehead against the glass, watching the Yamuna's sluggish filth dissolve into the Tungabhadra's gleam. A vendor wove through the aisles, hawking *kapi* in clay cups; the brew's bitterness curled against the metallic tang of anticipation. The wheels sang their own song—unfinished verses, unfinished verses—as Bangalore's skyline bloomed on the horizon, a concrete thicket crowned with coconut palms.

On Platform 1, Chandram stood waiting—a garish contrast to the station's Soviet-era gloom. His Maruti 800, a tomato-red relic battered by Bangalore's infamous potholes, overflowed with jasmine garlands—their fragrance so thick, even a stray dog sneezed.

"Saala!" Chandram bellowed, crushing Sagar in a rib-cracking embrace. *"Delhi turned you into a ghost! Look at these shoulders—bhindi stems have more muscle!"*

With a grunt, he heaved Sagar's trunk into the boot, sending a flurry of parking tickets and a *Playboy* magazine (1994 World Cup edition) fluttering to the floor.

As they lurched into MG Road's snarling traffic, the car radio blared *"Churake Dil Mera"*. Chandram's voice rose above it, a feverish ode to Bangalore's metamorphosis.

"That's where Samrat Hotel stood—gone! And that chutney dosa cart? Replaced by a Pizza Hut! Progress, yaar!"

Sagar clung to the door handle, the jasmine garlands wilting around his neck—a noose of nostalgia tightening with every mile.

ᗡᗡᗡ

Their friendship, once quiet, had grown wild—like monsoon weeds breaking through concrete, relentless and unshakable. Chandram, always the storyteller, led Sagar through Bangalore's chaos with the ease of a ringmaster. At Brigade Road's neon-lit pubs, Old Monk burned their throats as they devoured chaat, while engineers in Safari suits argued about microchips and Sagar scribbled haikus onto napkins. *"This city speaks in algorithms,"* he muttered once, watching a man debate resistor size over rum.

At K.C. Das, syrup dripped from soft *rosogollas* onto Chandram's Armani tie. *"This stain is a metaphor!"* he declared, dabbing at it with a tissue. *"Sweetness beats corporate greed!"* In Cubbon Park, Chandram swung a cricket bat like a businessman sealing a deal, while Sagar's bowling—erratic yet calculated—mirrored his tangled past. Bureaucrats' children jeered, but the squirrels, at least, seemed to cheer.

Rituals formed like sediment—layers of laughter and quiet defiance. Over masala dosas at Vidyarthi Bhavan, Chandram, calculator in hand, would theatrically accuse Sagar, *"Three mangoes in your veshti—caught! Even Principal Shastri's ghost wants a share!"* Their haiku battles were even fiercer, Chandram's dry wit—

"Boardroom deals
Monsoon leaks through ceiling cracks
Boss's toupee flies"

—against Sagar's quiet ache—

"Ledger dust blooms
A clerk's sigh becomes a storm
Peacock learns to drown."

The loser always paid for *bisi bele bath*. Sagar often lost.

Sagar's desk crouched beneath a window that framed Ulsoor Lake. Once, its waters had mirrored the endless stars of Vizag's coastline. Now, they reflected Bangalore's restless cranes, gnawing at the sky. A faded sticker clung stubbornly to the wood: *"Silence Please, Clerk at Work."*

And yet, silence never truly existed. Somewhere beyond the city's smog, he could still hear the ghost of Sandhya's *ghungroos*, their melody drowned beneath the relentless hum of factory machines.

ᐳᐳᐳ

Chandram's bungalow stood like the polished set of an old film—pristine, staged, almost too perfect. Every Sunday, Sagar arrived with oil-stained packets of Davangere *benne dosa*, the butter seeping through the paper like melted resolve. The dosas were an offering, a flimsy excuse for the dinners he had *"missed."* Chandram accepted them with an indulgent grin, swallowing both dosa and the unspoken.

Sandhya met him at the teakwood door, her smile a studied performance—her body frozen in *ardhamandali*, the half-sit stance of Bharatanatyam, as if caught between greeting and retreat.

Entrance: "Hi, Sagar."
Why? Because anything more would risk unraveling the careful

threads of normalcy.

She kept her gaze fixed on the *kolam* patterns, the rice flour swirls blurring under her breath. Her voice, once a melody that had carried across Vizag's beaches, was now a scratched long-play (LP), skipping over the same old grooves.

Exit: "Bye, Sagar."

Why? Because goodbye was easier than acknowledging everything in between.

In the space between those words, the past hummed—unspoken, unbearable.

Her hands trembled as she poured filter coffee into a steel tumbler, the *kumkum* on her forehead quivering like a dying ember. Sagar's fingers tightened around the cup, knuckles whitening, as if bracing against a cliff's edge. The heat seeped through the steel, but he didn't flinch—pain was a familiar, almost welcome, distraction.

Then, one monsoon afternoon, a moment of betrayal—accidental, cruel.

As Sandhya leaned forward to serve *vada*, the silk *pallu* of her saree slipped, revealing the silver chain around her neck—the twin of Sagar's. His breath caught. His fingers twitched, muscle memory almost guiding them to adjust her drape, just as he had once done before rehearsals.

But Chandram's laughter sliced through the air. *"Relax, yaar. She's not your audit file!"*

The joke sat between them, dense and suffocating. Sandhya's hands flew to her saree, the *pallu* hastily tucked back into place, her face carefully blank. Sagar looked down at his coffee, watching the liquid swirl—circles within circles, truth dissolving into a lie they had all agreed to drink.

And in the corner of the room, unnoticed yet ever-watchful, Renuka, the maid, took it all in. She was the unseen record-keeper of Chandram's house, her sharp eyes capturing every whisper, every glance, every misplaced tremor. In her mind, the memories were stacked neatly, like well-folded laundry—waiting for the day they would need to be unfurled.

Her memory was updated with happenings:

Saab's friend—Sagar Sir—came to drop papers. Saab was snoring in the study room, his breath rattling through the half-shut door. On the side table, Memsaab's college photo—laughing, younger, wrapped in a dance costume, ghungroos gleaming like new coins.

Sagar Sir stood there, staring.

Sweat patches bloomed under his arms, yaar, like he'd stolen something. I was dusting Lakshmi Devi's photo in its gold frame when I coughed. He jumped, hands twitching like a man caught red-handed.

"Just... admiring the frame."

Frame? Che! His eyes weren't on the frame. Later, I found his handkerchief crumpled near the sofa, stained with train smoke and something heavier—something like sadness.

Another Day:

Memsaab made toast, like always. Usually golden, crisp—like temple hundi coins. But today, Sagar Sir spoke of Vizag beaches.

"The waves there roar like tigers, Renuka!"

Her hand froze midair. The toast turned black, smoke curling like an omen. She stared at the toaster as if it had betrayed her.

"Sorry," she whispered. She fed the charred bread to the stray dog outside. It sniffed once, then walked away. Even animals know the taste of burnt love, nah?

Sagar Sir didn't eat. He sipped black coffee, staring at his spoon as if it held the past.

Saab only laughed. "Lee, you'll burn down Bangalore!"

But Memsaab's kumkum was smudged. Like she had cried in the pooja room again.

ᚦᚦᚦ

The afternoon sun hung low over Cubbon Park, spilling gold through the banyan trees, dappling the grass where Chandram lay sprawled. A half-finished Kingfisher beer dangled from his fingers, catching the light in lazy glints. Around them, Bangalore's noise softened to a hum—children chasing soap bubbles, vendors hawking bhel puri, office workers peeling off their ties like shed snakeskin.

Sagar sat cross-legged, plucking a dandelion from the earth. The fragile seeds trembled in the breeze, scattering like the syllables of a secret he'd sworn to bury.

"*Why no wife, yaar?*" Chandram prodded, squinting up at him. "*You're not that ugly.*" His tone was light, but the words landed like a stone in still water.

Sagar crushed the dandelion's stem between his fingers, its milky sap staining his thumb. "*Never found the right... rhythm,*" he murmured.

Rhythm. The word itself summoned her.

Sandhya's ghungroos had once kept time with his heartbeat, her laughter weaving through his silences.

Chandram snorted, rolling onto his side. "*Arre, marry a dancer! They love poets.*" He grinned, oblivious to the blade twisting in Sagar's chest. "*Find yourself a Mayuri. You'll write sonnets while she spins!*"

The peacock feather in Sagar's pocket—plucked from Vizag's shore years ago, its iridescent eye still flecked with sea salt—pressed against his thigh, a sharp rebuke. He had carried it like a talisman. Now, it felt like a shiv.

"*Dancers need more than sonnets,*" Sagar said, his voice fraying at the edges.

Chandram waved his beer, foam sloshing over his fingers. "*Nonsense! Women eat that filmy romance up. Roses, shayari, holding hands at Lalbagh—*"

A peacock's shrill cry cut through the air.

The bird strutted past, tail fanned in a defiant arc, its unblinking stare locking onto Sagar. For a single breath, the park stilled—laughter, traffic, the rustling trees all swallowed by the weight of that gaze.

Chandram chuckled, uneasy. "*Even the birds agree!*"

Sagar stood abruptly, brushing grass from his trousers. "*I should go. Files to sort.*"

"*Yaar, always working!*" Chandram lobbed a cashew at his retreating back. "*Live a little!*"

But Sagar was already walking. The feather's barb dug deeper, a crimson bead blooming through the fabric.

Behind him, the peacock screeched again—a sound like a soul tearing at the seams.

𝄞𝄞𝄞

The evening sun cast molten gold over Chandram's bungalow, its light slanting through the wide windows, stretching their shadows across the marble floor. Sandhya was out—her absence marked by a note on the fridge:

"Gone to Nritya Sanje. Back by 10."

Chandram poured two glasses of whiskey, the ice clinking like distant chimes. He handed one to Sagar with a grin.

"*Remember Principal Shastri's mango trees?*" he chuckled, sinking into his chair. "*You hid three in your veshti, you sly bastard.*"

Sagar forced a smile. "*And you tripped over your chappal, nearly got us caught.*"

They laughed, their voices filling the room with echoes of a time before life had grown complicated. The whiskey burned warm, loosening old knots, letting them slip into a rhythm of nostalgia. Between stories and slurred jokes, the bottle grew lighter.

Then, as if the night itself exhaled, their laughter faded into uneasy silence.

Chandram swirled his drink. "*Why haven't you married, yaar? Life's lonely without someone.*"

Sagar studied the amber liquid in his glass. "*Not everyone finds a soul mate in wife.*"

Something in Chandram's gaze shifted. "*You missed my wedding,*" he said, voice quieter now. "*People said... you lost someone in Vizag.*"

Sagar's throat tightened. Memories flooded back—salt-kissed beaches, a dancer's laughter, the chain that once hung around his neck.

Chandram leaned in. "*Was there a girl?*"

"*Yes,*" Sagar admitted, barely a whisper.

"*Do you still think of her?*"

"*Every day.*"

Chandram's grip tightened around his glass. "*What was her name?*"

The room seemed to shrink, the air thick with something neither of them could name.

"*Sandhya,*" Sagar murmured, exhaustion pressing heavy against his eyelids. "*She was a dancer.*"

The ice in Chandram's glass cracked. A fragile thing, breaking.

Outside, the city hummed—a distant honk, a street dog's bark, the rhythmic *thap* of a passing auto-rickshaw. But inside, time had frozen.

Sagar slumped back into the couch, the whiskey prying open vaults he'd sworn to keep sealed. His words came slow, like confessions unravelling in the dim light.

"*I loved her, Chandram,*" he whispered to the ceiling, the fan above spinning in lazy circles, as if chasing its own tail. "*But destiny... it's a bastard. Our castes—*" he exhaled sharply "*—they built a wall even the gods couldn't climb.*"

Chandram sat motionless; his whiskey untouched. The condensation pooled around the base of the glass, silent as withheld tears.

"*She deserved better,*" Sagar continued, his voice thick, raw. "*A life I couldn't give... jewels, a big house...*" His gaze flickered to Chandram. "*You.*" He let out a bitter laugh. "*But yaar, those moments... the beach, her laughter... they haunt me. Now she's just a ghost in a mangalsutra.*"

His head lolled back, the words dissolving into a drunken sigh. His empty glass slipped from his fingers, landing with a dull *thud* on the carpet. Within minutes, his breathing slowed, settling into the rhythm of sleep.

Chandram didn't move. His gaze shifted—first to Sagar, crumpled and unconscious, then to the wedding photo on the wall.

Sandhya, wrapped in red silk, *ghungroos* peeking from beneath the folds of her saree.

Her smile never quite reached her eyes.

His Sandhya.

Their Sandhya.

ᢒᢒᢒ

The jingle of *ghungroos* announced her return. Sandhya paused in the doorway, the silver chain at her throat catching the hallway light, flashing like a half-buried truth.

Chandram lay still, his breaths deliberately slow, feigning sleep. She hesitated—just for a moment—then slid into bed, her back a cold, unyielding wall between them.

Outside, a peacock screamed—a jagged, primal sound. The night itself seemed to unravel.

ᢒᢒᢒ

At dawn, Chandram's driver eased Sagar out of the car, guiding his unsteady steps toward his apartment. Whiskey still clung to his breath, last night's confessions lurking in the cracks of his consciousness.

The door groaned open. Sagar collapsed onto his bed, the morning light slicing through dusty windows, exposing the wreckage of memory. A dull, insistent pounding filled his skull. Flashes of the night clawed at him—Chandram's frozen stare, the name *Sandhya* spat into the air like a curse.

His stomach twisted. He stumbled to the bathroom, retching up bile and regret, then staggered back to his room.

On the nightstand, the peacock feather lay untouched, its iridescent eye staring, unblinking. Accusing.

ᢒᢒᢒ

Across the city, Chandram sat at his desk, eyes fixed on the office wall, yet seeing nothing. Sagar's words echoed louder than the factory machines, louder than the city's honks and hammering.

His fingers found the wedding album.

Page after page, Sandhya stared back at him—adorned, decorated, a bride made beautiful by expectation. Her coy glances. The practiced tilt of her smile. And then, a frame he had ignored before—her eyes in that precise moment when he'd clasped the *mangalsutra* around her neck.

Not joy.

Not nervous anticipation.

A flinch.

As if the weight of that sacred thread had burned.

Chandram closed the album. His hand lingered on the cover, fingers pressing into the past, trying to make sense of what had already been written.

Outside, in the smog-thickened sky, a lone peacock cried once more.

ppp

Why had she hidden Sagar? Why did her happiness look like a Bharatanatyam pose—perfect, poised, but lifeless?

Sandhya had spoken of her childhood in Vizag—the sting of her friend's death, the blisters from her first ghungroos, the stage fright that once stole her voice. She had gifted Chandram every shard of her past, each one polished, pristine—except the one that cut deepest: Sagar.

Chandram had mistaken her honesty for completeness. He had revelled in her stories, believing he knew her heart. But the night he observed the silver chain around her neck—its twin lying coiled in Sagar's velvet pouch—he understood.

Her truth had always been a Bharatanatyam performance. Every glance, every smile, every carefully placed emotion—a dance of grace, masking the tremor beneath.

The betrayal wasn't her silence. It was the illusion that there had been no locked doors in her heart. Now, every memory—the way her fingers tensed at Vizag's mention, the unshed tears she blamed on "dust"—became a lie wrapped in silk.

At their anniversary party, Chandram watched her dance. Her movements were flawless, her abhinaya impeccable, her smile a perfect crescent of devotion. But her eyes—her eyes were glazed with ghosts.

His Sandhya. A stranger spinning inside a gilded cage of her own making.

The chain around Sagar's neck—the one she had gifted him—suddenly felt like a betrayal.

ᗡᗡᗡ

Chandram sat in his parked car outside the factory, engine off but his mind roaring. The dashboard clock glowed 3:47 AM. He hadn't slept in days. Every time he closed his eyes, he saw them—Sagar's trembling hands, Sandhya's silver chain, the peacock feather left behind like a taunt.

If I ask Sandhya...
She might shatter. Or worse, confirm his dread—that her laughter at breakfast, her fingers laced with his at movies, her yes to his proposal—had all been a performance. That the woman he loved was a mural painted over cracks.

If I confront Sagar...
Would their decades of friendship dissolve into ash? Sagar, who had donated blood when Chandram's mother was hospitalised. Sagar, who had held him steady at his father's funeral. Now a stranger who had loved his wife in another lifetime.

Chandram had questions with no answers.

Does she still trace his name in her sleep?
When she dances, is it for me—or for the ghost of him?
Did I steal someone else's destiny?

But the worst part wasn't the betrayal. It was the *unknowing.* Love had been his compass, and now the needle spun wildly, directionless.

At dawn, he drove to Ulsoor Lake, where they'd once raced paper boats. The water mirrored Bangalore's smog—murky, unreadable. He thought of the choices before him.

Option 1: Storm the castle.
Barge into the house, hurl accusations, dissect every lie. Risk losing her forever.

Option 2: Bury the bones.

Play the fool. Let Sandhya's chain and Sagar's silence gather dust. Pretend his marriage isn't a mosaic of half-truths.

Option 3: Wait.

Watch. Does she still glance at the clock when Sagar leaves? Does his laughter falter when she enters?

But deep down, he fears the answer to the one question he can't voice:

Was I ever her choice, or just her compromise?

He starts the car. For now, he'll take the long route home—past the florist where he bought her roses, the theatre where they kissed in the back row, the temple where she had prayed for their future.

Let the truth wait, he tells himself. *Let me love her a little longer.*

ᑭᑭᑭ

Chandram stood at the edge of their bedroom balcony, the Bangalore night humming with distant traffic and the metallic scent of impending rain. Inside, Sandhya slept, her breath steady, the silver chain at her throat catching stray slivers of moonlight. He gripped the railing, his knuckles whitening, as if he could crush the questions festering in his mind.

What lives in the silence between us?

He replayed every moment like a cursed film reel:

At dinner, her laughter had faltered when he mentioned Sagar's promotion.

His friend left rooms too quickly now, his jokes brittle, his eyes never meeting Chandram's for more than a heartbeat.

The chain—always there, coiled around her neck like a serpent guarding Lord Shiva.

He had begun cataloguing lies:

"I'm tired," when her eyes reddened.

"Work stress," when Sagar cancelled their weekend cricket match.

"Old friend," when he found the faded peacock feather in her diary.

To ask Sandhya was to risk the fragile ecosystem of their marriage—the shared jokes, the Sunday rituals, the way she still warmed his side of the bed. *What if the truth was a grenade? What if she said, "Yes, I loved him. I still do"?*

To confront Sagar was to sever the last thread of a 20-year friendship. Sagar, who had once taken a beating for him in school. Sagar, who had always been the one to stay.

Chandram found himself trapped in their past, searching for hidden truths.

The wedding album—Sandhya smiling, but her eyes distant.
Sagar's transfer letter—dated just a week before the wedding. Coincidence?
The locked drawer—where she kept her Bharatanatyam costumes, the key long gone.

He had become an archaeologist of his own life, uncovering relics of betrayal.

One midnight, drunk on smuggled brandy, he typed a text to Sagar:
Meet me. We need to talk.
He deleted it.

Another night, he shook Sandhya awake, the words clawing his throat—*Do you love him?*
Her sleepy murmur disarmed him: *"You're my husband."*
Not *No.* Not *Never.*

So, Chandram began leaving clues, testing their reactions.

He casually mentioned Vizag's beaches—*Sandhya dropped a teacup.*
He gifted Sagar a handkerchief embroidered with a peacock—*Sagar never used it.*
He played *Chura Ke Dil Mera*, their old college anthem—*Sandhya quietly left the room.*

But he never pushed further.

At the Diwali party, he watched them—Sandhya resplendent in gold, Sagar nursing a drink in the corner. Their eyes met across the room—a flicker of something ancient and aching—before they looked away.

Chandram laughed too loudly, clinked glasses with some friends, and pretended not to notice.

That night, he dreamt of peacocks. They circled him, screaming, their feathers sharp as knives.

When he woke, Sandhya's side of the bed was cold.

In the living room, she sat by the window, the chain in her fist, staring at the moon.

He didn't ask.

Past Shadows, Present Lights

Chandram folded the last of his clothes and zipped up his suitcase. The metallic click of the lock echoed through the quiet room. Sandhya stood by the window; her arms wrapped around herself as if shielding against an invisible storm. Her eyes brimmed with unshed tears, her silence louder than words.

"*I will miss you so much, Chandu,*" she whispered, her voice carrying the weight of an unspoken plea.

Chandram stepped forward and gently kissed her forehead. "*I'll be back soon, Mayuri.*"

It had been weeks since he had called her that. A ghost of a smile played on her lips, but the emptiness in her heart deepened. He had always been her anchor, her strength, the reason behind her small joys. Now, as he prepared to leave, a strange unease settled within her.

"*What do you want from Bombay?*" he asked, forcing a smile, masking the turmoil within.

"*Take care of your health and call me daily… What else would I ask for?*" Her voice cracked as a single tear traced a slow path down her cheek.

He pulled her into a tight embrace, as if memorizing her warmth. A lone tear escaped his eye, but he wiped it away before it betrayed him. Chandram was never one to show vulnerability.

The day before, he had spoken to Renuka. He had entrusted her with the responsibility of keeping an eye on things in his absence. Who came to the house? With whom did Sandhya speak? Where did she go? He wanted to know everything. Not out of jealousy, but to find an answer that tormented his soul—did Sandhya still love Sagar?

If she did, he would let her go, without a second thought. He had loved her too much to imprison her heart.

As his car pulled away towards the airport, Sandhya stood at the doorstep, watching the fading taillights. A part of her longed to run after him, but she simply clutched her dupatta tighter and turned back into the house.

ppp

The tain to Bombay was smooth, but Chandram's heart was racing. His hotel room was painted in shades of grey, mirroring his state of mind. He called Sandhya as soon as he checked in, and she picked up on the first ring.

She spoke for an hour that night—something unusual for her. She narrated every tiny detail of her plans in his absence, her dance rehearsals, and even a cultural organization's request for her to perform for charity. But she never mentioned Sagar.

He expected that.

So, after their call ended, he dialled Renuka. The first three days passed without incident. But on the fourth day, Sagar visited.

Renuka relayed every detail—the way they greeted each other formally, the way their words lacked emotion, but their eyes held something unspoken.

A week later, Sagar visited again. This time, they went to the temple together, with Renuka in tow. There was nothing unusual—just two people who shared a past, now interacting with respect and careful distance.

Yet, Chandram wasn't at peace.

ppp

One night, it rained heavily. Sagar, drenched to the bone, sought shelter in Sandhya's house. She handed him a towel and one of Chandram's shirts while Renuka silently prepared food. That night, they all slept in separate rooms.

But in the dead of the night, Sagar woke up and wandered into the veranda. The storm had calmed outside, but inside, something stirred. He walked towards Sandhya's room... and then stopped. He turned back, shaking his head at his own weakness.

At that moment, Sandhya opened her door.

Their eyes met.

They climbed up to the terrace, where the wind whispered secrets between them. Silence stretched, heavy and suffocating, until Sandhya spoke.

"Why?"

"I don't know," Sagar sighed. *"I just wanted to see the Mayuri I once knew. Does Chandram know about us?"*

"I never told him."

"He's a good man."

"Yes. He treats me with great respect."

"I still miss you."

"I miss you too... But we shouldn't talk like this. I don't want to be the reason two best friends turn into enemies."

"You won't be," Sagar reassured. *"I'm not a fool to want my best friend's wife. You're just a memory now. One that haunts me, but no longer belongs to me."*

A bitter smile crossed Sandhya's lips. *"I wish we had the life we dreamed of."*

"Life has a cruel sense of humour," he replied. *"Did you search for me at your wedding?"*

"I waited for you."

"I wasn't there. I couldn't bear to watch."

"I'm sorry, Sagar. I hurt you so much."

"You didn't. I just wasn't worthy of you. Chandram was. And you're where you deserve to be."

She held his hand for a brief moment. *"You deserve peace, Sagar. And one day, you'll find it."*

Lightning flashed, breaking their trance. They hurried back inside, retreating into their separate spaces, carrying with them the ghosts of a love that could never be.

Renuka, hidden in the shadows, had heard everything. The next morning, she called Chandram. He listened in silence, then abruptly cut the call.

He had made a terrible mistake.

ᐳᐳᐳ

That evening, he called Sandhya. *"I'll be home in a week."*

Her joy was palpable, and yet, he could hear the weight of the days they had spent apart.

A week later, he knocked on Sagar's door. Sagar opened it, surprised to see him. Before he could say a word, Chandram pulled him into a hug.

"I'm sorry, my friend."

Sagar stood frozen, unsure how much Chandram knew. But as the weight of the words settled in, his eyes softened. They spoke briefly, but Chandram's heart was lighter. He asked Sagar to keep this moment a secret from Sandhya. She didn't need to know that he had ever doubted her.

Then, he went home.

Sandhya ran into his arms, tears rolling down her face. He kissed her, passionately, deeply. She wept because she had missed him. He wept for a different reason.

But their love erased the difference.

That night, he told Renuka never to mention anything again. She nodded, understanding his heart.

Life returned to normal. Sagar remained their friend, visiting often, laughing over old memories. And Chandram learned a valuable lesson—love is not just about trust, but about the courage to let go of doubt.

The Last Dance

The wedding hall shimmered with golden lights, the air thick with the scent of jasmine and sandalwood. Laughter rang from every corner, the sounds of music and celebration drowning out the whispers of old wounds.

Sagar stood at the mandap, dressed in ivory silk, the sacred fire painting his face in flickering hues of orange and gold. His bride—Meera—sat beside him, her eyes bright with trust, her smile untouched by the ghosts of the past. She was everything he had never dared to ask for—gentle, kind, beautiful.

Chandram and Sandhya watched from the front row; their hands entwined in a silent understanding. When Sagar sought their blessings, Chandram embraced him like a brother, no words needed—only the weight of years between them. Sandhya placed a small kumkum dot on Meera's forehead, her fingers lingering for just a second longer, as if sealing a prayer.

Later that night, after the rituals had ended and the laughter had softened into the murmurs of guests departing, Sandhya found Sagar alone by the temple steps. The glow of the oil lamps flickered against the quiet night, casting shadows long and uncertain.

She stood beside him, their reflections wavering in the temple pond.

"You got your peace," she said softly.

Sagar exhaled, as if he had been holding his breath for years.

"And you?" he asked.

Sandhya smiled, but it was the kind of smile that belonged to old scars, not fresh wounds.

"We all find our ways to live," she whispered.

For a moment, neither spoke. Only the rustling of the banyan leaves filled the silence, carrying away the last remnants of what once was.

Then, Sandhya stepped back.

"Be happy, Sagar."

She turned and walked away, her silver chain catching the moonlight one last time before disappearing into the night.

As the wedding lamps dimmed and the night settled into silence, fate quietly rearranged its pieces.

Sagar found his lost love in Meera. Sandhya found hers in Chandram.

And at last, the past let them go.

3

Fallen Wings

Love isn't always a fairytale. Sometimes, it begins with a promise but takes a turn no one sees coming.

With time, distance becomes a reality.

Some loves fade.

Some loves wait.

And some come back when you least expect them to.

This is not just a love story.

This is a story of love, loss, and the choices that change everything.

Two Prime Numbers

Morning mist covered the tin roofs of Prem's neighbourhood like thin spiderwebs. The air smelled of wet soil and the jasmine flowers growing in his mother's small garden. Their one-story house stood in a maze of narrow lanes, where the sounds of daily life—clattering dishes, coughing, and the sizzle of cooking—had already begun. Inside, Prem's father sat in the kitchen, sipping bitter tea, his cough a reminder of years working in a dusty factory. Nearby, Prem's mother packed his lunch: warm flatbreads, spicy mango pickle, and a sweet *burfi* she tucked in for good luck.

Prem's room was orderly and quiet. His university blazer hung neatly beside his bed, and his old laptop sat on the desk, its screen filled with lines of code he'd written late into the night. The computer buzzed softly, a steady hum that matched Prem's determination to build a future far beyond the cramped lanes of his hometown.

Prem's room was neat and organized, like a carefully arranged museum. His textbooks stood in tidy piles, sorted by size. On the wall hung a framed photo of his school friends, their smiles frozen in time, as if cheering him on silently.

Prem dressed with care every morning, smoothing his crisp white shirt and adjusting the silver watch his parents had given him as a gift for scoring the highest marks in his exams. *"This college will be your launchpad,"* his father had told him, voice swelling with pride. Prem touched the watch gently, a reminder of his family's hopes—and his own dreams of soaring far beyond the small world he knew.

The college bus pulled up in a puff of smoke, its worn-out seats already packed with students. Prem hurried to his spot by the window, plugged in his earphones, and played old songs softly. As the bus moved, the busy market lanes faded, replaced by wide-open fields glowing under the morning sun.

Golden sunlight spread over the rice fields outside. Prem scribbled in his notebook—jotted down math problems, circled scholarship dates, and even drew a tiny rocket in the corner. He was so focused that he didn't notice the girls sitting a few rows back, whispering and laughing among themselves.

Mounika's hostel room felt damp and lonely. The walls were covered in old, peeling purple paint, and a rusty fan creaked as it spun slowly above her narrow bed. The mattress was thin and uncomfortable, as if it carried the weight of all her regrets. She had arrived at the hostel a week before classes started, desperate to escape her hometown—a place where every street and corner reminded her of the boy who had sworn to love her forever, then disappeared without a word.

At the bus station, her father had handed her a small statue of Lord Ganesha, the Hindu god of new beginnings. "Start fresh," he'd urged her. But Mounika couldn't bring herself to believe in new beginnings. She placed the idol on her windowsill, turning its face toward the wall, as though even hope was too painful to look at.

Mounika found comfort in books. Her desk overflowed with them: poetry by Rumi, old Russian novels with folded pages, and a sketchbook where she drew broken lines—faces without smiles, angry oceans, and angels with missing wings. These stories and sketches were her escape, a way to bury memories of the past she couldn't fix.

The only thing she allowed herself to enjoy was a small jasmine plant near her window. Its sweet smell fought bravely against the damp, gloomy air of her room. To Mounika, the jasmine was more than a flower—it was a tiny, stubborn hope that maybe, someday, light could find its way into her world.

That morning, Mounika wore a black *salwar kameez*—a long tunic with loose pants—and draped a white *chunni* over her shoulders. Her hands shook as she braided her hair, the mirror reflecting her anxious eyes. The dining hall's noise—clanging plates, loud chatter—overwhelmed her. She grabbed an apple and slipped into the quiet courtyard, where she could breathe again.

From the courtyard, she watched college buses pull in, students pouring out like colourful confetti, laughing and hugging. Mounika bit into the apple, its tartness sharp on her tongue, and wondered if she would ever feel as bright and unbroken as they seemed. The courtyard walls felt like they were closing in, echoing the loneliness she carried in her chest.

The computer science classroom buzzed with nervous chatter as freshmen settled in. Sunlight filtered through dusty windows, lighting up flecks of chalk floating in the air. Prem sat confidently in the front row, pen ready, eyes fixed on the professor. Meanwhile, Mounika lingered near the door, clutching her notebook tightly. With all seats taken except one at the very back, she slid into the last bench, shoulders hunched as if trying to disappear.

The first class was mostly introductions—students sharing names and hometowns, forming quick friendships. During the break, the room erupted with laughter as groups swapped stories and jokes. Prem was soon surrounded by classmates, his easy smile drawing them in. Mounika stayed silent, scribbling in her notebook, her eyes darting to the lively clusters around her. The gap between their worlds felt as wide as the classroom itself.

When Mounika slid into the seat beside Prem, their shoulders brushed lightly. He turned, and she caught the faint scent of sandalwood and citrus—maybe his soap? "Hi, I'm Prem," he said, his voice warm but gentle, as if he sensed her shyness. She nodded, eyes fixed on the coding examples projected on the board, before slipping away after class. But the next period, she found herself sitting beside him again, drawn by some unspoken pull.

The professor assigned a coding task: *"Write a program to list prime numbers below 50. Work in pairs!"* Mounika's mind went blank, her notebook page starkly empty. Prem nudged his notes toward her—neat lines of code, arrows linking ideas. "Start with a nested loop," he said, pointing at her screen. His fingertip grazed her hand, sending a jolt through her. She typed shakily, guided by his calm instructions, her panic slowly melting into focus. Around them, chatter and laughter faded as numbers filled her screen—lonely primes, perfect and unbroken.

His patience unravelled her. She typed a shaky for *i in range(2,50):*

"Good," he murmured, and something in his tone—not praise, but quiet respect—made her breath catch.

By the end of class, their code ran flawlessly. Prem glanced at her sketchbook, left open to a page of inky wings. "You draw?"

She snapped it shut. "No."

But as they filed out, he lingered. "Mounika, right? The professor took attendance."

She froze. He remembered.

Before she could reply, his friends swarmed him—backslaps, jokes about his "nerd aura"—and she melted into the crowd, her heart a wild, confused thing.

Prem couldn't sleep that night. His mind replayed moments from the day—how Mounika had tensed when their hands accidentally touched, how her eyes darted away whenever he spoke. He wondered about the sketches in her notebook, those dark, broken lines that seemed to whisper secrets she wouldn't share.

On his desk, his coding notebook lay open. Between neat rows of formulas and diagrams, a rough drawing of wings now filled the margin—awkwardly drawn, but full of quiet longing. Prem traced the lines with his finger, unsure why her guarded heart had etched itself so deeply into his.

Mounika sat by her hostel window, staring at the jasmine plant glowing faintly under the moonlight. Its petals seemed to hold the night's silence like secrets. She opened her sketchbook to the page of wings—the ones she'd drawn months ago, jagged and unfinished—and paused. Then, in small, careful letters, she wrote beside them: *for i in range(2,50):* the first line of the code Prem had taught her that day.

Below it, she added the code for finding prime numbers. Those lonely, stubborn digits that could only be divided by themselves and one. The jasmine's scent drifted in, mixing with the ink on the page. For a moment, it didn't smell like her ex's lies or her father's hopeful idol. It smelled like Prem's sandalwood soap, like nested loops and quiet patience. She shut the book quickly, as if afraid the words might flutter away like the wings she'd never dare to finish.

for i in range(2,50):
if all(i % j != 0 for j in range(2, i)):
print(i)

Prime numbers. Lonely, indivisible, perfect.

New Friendship

After sunset, Mounika's hostel hallway turned eerie. Flickering fluorescent lights cast shaky shadows on the walls, and the creak of bunk beds mixed with muffled cries from behind closed doors. The air felt heavy, as if the building itself was sighing with the weight of lonely nights and whispered secrets.

But Mounika's room, lit by a small desk lamp, became her home. Here, she lost herself in sketches—Prem's hands (rough fingertips, a silver ring glinting), tangled lines of code that looked like math turned into art, and wings. Always wings: broken, mended, or halfway to the sky. The lamp's golden glow made the pages of her sketchbook feel alive, as if her pencil could rewrite the world outside her door.

At 10:03 p.m., her phone buzzed.

Prem: *Saw your sketchbook in class. Why wings?*

She hesitated, then typed: *They're heavy. Can't fly, but can't drop them either.*

Prem: *Like dead code. Takes up memory but doesn't run.*

She smiled. Their conversations were bridges between worlds—hers of metaphors, his of logic. Nights bled into hours of texts:

- He sent photos of his journals, equations curled like poetry.

- She recited Rumi verses, her voice timid in voice notes.

- He confessed he'd never read fiction; she mailed him her battered copy of *The God of Small Things* with underlined passages.

"*You're awake?*" he called once at midnight, his voice hushed. The hostel Wi-Fi crackled.

"*Always,*" she said, curled under her blanket.

"*Tell me something real.*"

She paused. "*I hate the smell of jasmine. It's what he—my ex—wore.*"

Silence. Then, "*I'll burn my sandalwood soap.*"

"*Don't. I... like yours.*"

ᐅᐅᐅ

Mounika first noticed Prabha in the hostel dining hall—a whirlwind of confidence in a leather jacket and combat boots, her laughter slicing through the clatter of steel plates. Prabha's eyes, lined with kohl sharp enough to draw blood, locked onto Mounika's solitary figure hunched over a cold paratha. "You," she declared, sliding into the bench across from her, "look like a haunted library. Sit with us. Loneliness is *badtameez* here."

"Us" meant Prabha's entourage: three girls with the same smudged eyeliner and bitten-lipped smirks, their nails painted black as crow feathers. They held court over steaming cups of chai, dissecting campus scandals with the precision of surgeons.

"*Mounika's too... funeral,*" Prabha announced, waving a dismissive hand. "*You're Mona now. Less tragic, more...*" She snapped her fingers, eyeing Mounika's faded salwar kameez. "*Alive.*"

By sunset, Prabha had rewritten Mona's DNA:

"Burn those widow kurtas. Jeans. Now."

"Library? Boring. We're crashing the frat party—*with* vodka."

"Block that coding monk. Boys like him? Heart-hoarders."

The jasmine plant sagged on Mounika's windowsill, its once-vibrant petals now brittle and brown, as if Prabha's presence had leached the life from it. Mona—*not Mounika, never Mounika anymore*—stared at it absently while Prabha painted her lips a violent red, the tube of stolen lipstick trembling in her unsteady grip. "*Perfect,*" Prabha crooned, smudging the edges deliberately. "Now you look *alive.*" The clove cigarettes she chain-smoked left a hazy film in the air, their acrid smoke mingling with the rot of the dying jasmine.

Prabha's disdain for Prem wasn't just words—it was a living, snarling creature. At lunch, she snatched Mona's phone mid-bite, her eyes narrowing at the screen.

Prem: Need help debugging the AI project? Coffee after class?

"*Friends?*" Prabha sneered, her voice a serrated blade. She jerked Mona's chin toward the courtyard, where Prem stood surrounded by admirers, demonstrating a drone that whirred like a metallic dragonfly. His grin was easy, his hands gesturing wildly as the crowd leaned in.

"See that? He's a virus—infects every girl with his 'genius' act. You're just another line in his code."

Mona's chest tightened. Prem's laughter drifted through the canteen windows, warm and unguarded, so unlike the brittle giggles Prabha's group practiced like a sacrament.

That night, Prabha stormed into her room, reeking of clove smoke and vodka.

"We're watching a movie," she announced, snatching Mona's wrist. Her nails bit crescent moons into the skin.

"And you're deleting his number. Now."

"I—I have an assignment—"

"Assignment?" Prabha's laugh was a bark. *"You'll fail life if you keep orbiting that narcissist."*

Mona's phone lit up—**Prem: Saw a starling today. Its wings reminded me of your sketch. Still think they're heavy?**

The words blurred. For a heartbeat, Mona imagined replying—*Tell me about the starling. Tell me about wings.* But Prabha's grip tightened, her breath hot and sour. *"Delete. Him."*

Mona's finger hovered over the screen. Outside, the starling Prem had mentioned roosted in the jasmine's skeletal branches, its feathers iridescent under the streetlamp.

The calls became a relentless tide, crashing against the walls Mounika had built:

Prem (11:14 p.m.):*You missed the coding meet. Everything okay?*
Seen.

Prem (12:02 a.m.):*Sivani said you're avoiding me. Why?*
Seen.

Prem (1:17 a.m.):*Mounika. Please.*

The glow of her phone etched shadows on the hostel ceiling. Mounika's thumbs hovered, trembling, as she typed and erased replies like cursed incantations:

I'm scared (too raw).
They say you're a liar (too weak).

I don't know what's real anymore (too true).

She buried her face in the pillow, its fabric soaking up silent tears. The jasmine plant's skeletal remains rattled in the breeze, a brittle chorus to her guilt.

The moon hung low, a silver coin wedged in the sky. Mounika's finger hovered over *unblock*, her breath shallow. His profile photo—a pixelated sketch *she'd* drawn of the banyan tree, its roots tangled like veins—flashed onto the screen. The memory ambushed her: Prem's laugh as she shaded the bark, his shoulder brushing hers, the world reduced to graphite and sunlight.

She pressed *call*.

He answered before the first ring faded. "Hey." A single syllable, frayed with sleepless nights.

"I..." Her voice cracked, the word dissolving.

Click. The hostel door flew open.

"*Mona!*" Prabha's voice slashed through the dark, sharp as shattered glass. She loomed in the doorway, backlit by the hall's jaundiced light, a clove cigarette dangling from her lips. "*Who're you—*"

The phone slipped from Mounika's grip, clattering to the floor. Prabha's boot descended, heel grinding the screen into a spiderweb of fractures.

"*Pathetic,*" Prabha spat, smoke curling from her nostrils like a dragon's wrath. "*Still tethered to that liar?*"

Mounika stared at the shattered device, Prem's voice still tinny and distant: "*Hello? Mounika? Are you—?*"

Prabha stomped once. Silence.

ϸϸϸ

At dawn, Mounika found a folded paper slipped under her door—a coding puzzle Prem had solved, his note scribbled in green ink:

for i in range(2, 50):
if all(i % j != 0 for j in range(2, i)):
print(i)

    # Prime numbers. Like us. Indivisible.

She pressed it to her chest, tears smudging the ink, as Prabha's laughter echoed down the hall.

What to do?

It happened under the banyan tree, its gnarled roots cradling shadows like ancient secrets. Prem's hands trembled as he handed Mounika a folded paper—a charcoal sketch he'd drawn, its lines swirling into a flock of birds ascending through storm clouds toward a sliver of sun.

"*It's... how I see you,*" he said, voice fraying at the edges. "*How you turn grey skies into something... alive.*"

Mounika traced the paper, her reflection fractured in the dim afternoon light. The strokes were deliberate, each shadow and curve a silent testament to nights he'd spent studying the tilt of her head, the way she bit her lip when lost in thought. Her ex's ghost hissed in her ear: "*You'll trust again? After me?*"

"*Prem, I...*" Her throat tightened.

He stepped back, hands raised as if surrendering. "*You don't have to say anything.*"

But his eyes begged. She folded the sketch, the crease cutting through the heart of the storm, leaving the birds forever suspended mid-flight. "*I'm not ready.*"

ϸϸϸ

Prabha's dominance thickened like monsoon clouds. She hijacked Mounika's weekends with "sisterhood rituals"—slathering avocado masks on their faces in her cramped dorm, blaring Punjabi hip-hop loud enough to drown out the world, while Mounika's phone buzzed with ignored pleas:

Prem (8:07 p.m.):*The group's presenting our lit analysis tomorrow. Could use your notes.*

Prem (9:13 p.m.):*Never mind. We'll wing it.*

When Mounika once murmured Prem's name, Prabha flicked her forehead, leaving a sticky smear of green clay. "*Uske liye itna pagal?* He's probably reciting Shakespeare to that artsy fresher, Preeti."

At 2 a.m., Mounika would lie awake, tracing the cracks in the ceiling, replaying Prem's confession under the banyan tree—the sketch of birds straining toward sunlight. Her finger hovered over his contact. *What if I—*

Prabha's fist hammered the door, her voice a serrated edge. *"Up! Come on girls. Its weekend!!"*

By week's end, the jasmine plant stood skeletal, its last petals scattered like unsent letters.

ᗡᗡᗡ

Preethi arrived at the hostel like a sunbeam cutting through monsoon gloom. A first-year arts student, she wore her warmth in the crinkle of her eyes and the dimpled smile that disarmed even the surliest seniors. Her laughter echoed in the stairwells, her paint-splattered dupatta trailing behind her like a comet's tail. She carried sketchbooks filled with watercolour galaxies and thrifted novels with dog-eared pages, her presence a quiet antidote to the hostel's brooding energy.

When ragging season began, Preethi became a target. Seniors cornered her in the courtyard, demanding she sing a song. Prem, passing by froze at the sound of her shaky voice. Without thinking, he stepped in, his tone polite but firm.

"She's here to study, not perform. Let her go."

The seniors sneered but retreated, unnerved by the quiet steel in his eyes.

"Thank you," Preethi whispered, clutching her frayed tote. *"I'm Preethi."*

"Prem. Let me walk you back."

Their friendship bloomed in small acts:

Prem carried her canvases to the art studio.

Preethi left him doodles of robots wearing flower crowns, tucked into his textbooks.

When hostel Wi-Fi died, he hotspot his phone so she could submit her online portfolio.

But it was Preethi's kindness that disarmed Mounika. One evening, she paused at Mounika's open door, drawn by the wings sketched on her wall. *"These are stunning,"* she said, her voice soft as charcoal dust. *"Like they're trying to escape the paper."*

Mounika stiffened, but Preethi didn't push. She simply left a sprig of jasmine from the campus garden on Mounika's desk—a silent offering.

Prabha, of course, noticed.

"That artsy beggars after your nerd," she sneered, painting Mounika's nails blood-red. *"Pathetic, how she throws smiles like loose change."*

But Mounika watched Preethi in the courtyard one dawn, sketching the sunrise with a reverence that made her chest ache. She wondered what it felt like to hold joy so lightly, to trust the world enough to paint it in gold.

ᛈᛈᛈ

The campus buzzed with whispers whenever Prem and Preethi walked together. Their friendship, bright and unguarded, became a spectacle. Prem carried her art supplies to the studio, his laughter mingling with hers as she teased him about his "engineer uniform" of ironed shirts and mismatched socks. Preethi doodled caricatures of him as a knight with a protractor shield, slipping them into his textbooks. To outsiders, it looked like romance—their banter too easy, their smiles too warm.

But they had rules:

No late-night calls.

No lingering touches.

No promises.

"People are staring again," Preethi muttered once, nodding toward a group of girls giggling behind their hands.

Prem shrugged. *"Let them. We know the truth."*

Yet the truth felt fragile. During a college fest, Preethi tripped onstage, and Prem caught her mid-fall, her hands gripping his shoulders, his arms circling her waist. A photo spread like wildfire:

Campus Couple's Dramatic Rescue! Mounika saw it on Prabha's phone, her stomach twisting as Prabha crowed, "*See? Even his hero act is recycled.*"

Mounika told herself she trusted Prem. But trust crumbled under the weight of Prabha's disdain and the hostel's gossip. She began mapping routes to avoid him—taking the back stairs, skipping the canteen, burying herself in the library's farthest corner.

One evening, she stumbled upon Prem and Preethi in the courtyard. Preethi was teaching him to sketch, her hand guiding his over the paper.

"*Loosen your grip,*" she laughed. "*It's not a coding problem.*"

Mounika froze. Prem's smile—the one that once lit up their late-night talks—now belonged to someone else. Prabha's voice hissed in her mind: "*You're just his backup code.*"

When Prem spotted her, his eyes widened. "*Mounika, wait—!*"

She fled, her chest burning.

Prem's texts piled up, unanswered:

Why are you avoiding me?

Did I do something wrong?

Please talk to me.

He cornered her once outside the hostel, his voice raw. "*Is this because of Preethi? We're just friends.*"

Mounika's throat tightened. She wanted to scream, *I know!* But Prabha's warnings echoed louder: "*You'll look desperate. Let him chase you.*"

"*I'm... busy,*" she lied, staring at his shoes.

The hurt in his eyes mirrored her own.

Preethi noticed. "*Fix this,*" she urged Prem, shoving him toward Mounika's usual bench.

"*She's drowning, and you're both too stubborn to throw a rope.*"

But Mounika had already retreated into Prabha's world—a blur of forced laughter and clove-scented nights. The jasmine plant, now just a brittle stem, gathered dust on her sill.

At the hostel's Diwali party, Preethi pulled Mounika aside. "*He misses you, you know.*"

Mounika stiffened. "*Why do you care?*"

"*Because you do.*" Preethi's voice softened. "*And because real friends don't let friends die of stupid pride.*"

But Prabha's hand clamped onto Mounika's wrist. "*Move, Mona. The losers' club is waiting.*"

As Preethi walked away, Mounika caught Prem's gaze across the room—a silent plea tangled in the smoke and noise. She turned her back, her heart a crumpled sketch of wings and *what-ifs*.

Destiny awaits...

The confession happened under an old banyan tree, its branches heavy with monsoon rain. Water collected in the cracks of the bark, like the tears on Mounika's face as she whispered, *"I love you."*

Prem stood still, stunned. Months ago, he'd given her a drawing of birds fighting through a storm here—his quiet wish for her to see herself as strong and brave. Now, her voice shook like those paper birds in the wind.

Then he smiled—a warm, glowing smile that cut through the dark like sunrise after a long night. He hugged her tightly, his arms a safe place from the rain. For a moment, nothing else existed—just the sound of rain, the smell of jasmine in her hair, and the truth of her words sinking deep into his heart.

But the next morning, nothing changed. Mounika fell back into the routine of Prabha's world. Her days melted into nights at brightly lit hostel parties, where clove cigarette smoke mixed with loud laughter that felt sharp and painful to Prem. She sat on sticky bar stools, drinking colourful cocktails. Prabha pushed into her hand, her eyes wandering to her buzzing phone in her bag—**Prem (9:02 p.m.): Walk by the lake?** —before she ignored it. At cafés, she pretended to care about gossip, her fingers touching the edge of her teacup where Prem had once kissed her. Her love for him stayed hidden, like a locket hidden under her clothes, cold and heavy.

ᑭᑭᑭ

Prem's hope faded like flowers under a harsh sun. His texts to Mounika piled up— **"Coffee?" "Found your lemon candies." "Just talk to me."**—each one feeling as pointless as tossing pebbles into a bottomless well. He lingered near the library steps where they'd once discussed poetry, now filled with strangers. At night, he replayed her *"I love you,"* in his mind wondering if it was temporary or a mistake. One evening, he saw her arm-in-arm with Prabha, their shadows merging into one dark shape. He turned away, the lemon candies in his pocket now melted into a sticky lump—a truth he ignored.

ϸϸϸ

By their final semester, Prem's hope was a dying spark. He swapped late-night talks for job applications, guarding his heart with spreadsheets and salary lists. He avoided cafeterias to escape Mounika's empty laughter echoing behind Prabha. Even the banyan tree felt haunted, its shadows whispering her confession—now a phrase that felt wrong, like a sentence missing some words. He packed his wing sketches into a shoebox, burying them under textbooks like a memory he couldn't keep.

Prem's voice cut through the clove-scented smoke, steady but sharp. *"You said you loved me."* His eyes, usually warm and focused, now stormy and hurt. *"Was that just... a lie?"* The library's dim light lit Mounika's face, shadows under her eyes—eyes that once sparkled for him but now looked tired and lost. She hugged herself, her party dress glittering faintly in the dark, like she was playing a part she couldn't stop.

"I meant it," she whispered, voice breaking. *"But I... don't know how to love."* She glanced at Prabha, who stood nearby like a hawk waiting to strike. *"Not with her—"* Her words faded into a shaky breath. Prem stepped closer, the air tense with all the messages he'd never sent and the plans she'd cancelled. *"Choose,"* he said, voice cracking. *"Her or me."*

The night after their last exam, Prem found Mounika outside the library. Prabha's cigarette glowed orange, smoke blurring Mounika's face as she leaned against a graffiti-covered wall. The air smelled of spice and burnt coffee. *"We need to talk,"* Prem said, voice steady but eyes shaky. Mounika tensed, glancing at Prabha, who blew a smoke ring and sneered, *"Enough drama. Mona, the cab's here."* Mounika hesitated, lips parted, but Prabha yanked her arm, dragging her toward the waiting car. Prem stood frozen under the library's harsh lights, her whispered *"I'm sorry"* swallowed by the engine's roar and her silence feeling like a typo that ruined the whole story of them.

ৡৡৡ

Rain hammered against the train windows as Prem shoved his suitcase inside. It held pieces of his old life—old engineering books, a faded sweatshirt that smelled of libraries, and a framed drawing of wings Mounika had made, its glass smudged from nights he'd stared at it, missing her. The train jerked forward, wheels clattering like his racing heart. Through the foggy glass, he imagined her—Mounika, a blur in a black kurta, Prabha gripping her arm tightly. Raindrops clung to her lashes like tears she wouldn't let fall.

Their goodbye felt like a fake performance. Mounika handed Prem a book of promises, her smile as forced as her *"Good luck."* Prabha stood nearby, smirking, her nails digging sharply into Mounika's arm. Prem wanted to yell, *"You picked her over me!"* But he stayed silent, just nodding, thinking of the promises that were left by her to be forgotten.

ৡৡৡ

Bhubaneswar greeted Prem with a mix of old traditions and new ambitions. Every morning, the loud bells of Lingaraj Temple rang out, competing with the quiet buzz of office buildings. Prem's cubicle was a plain box of bright lights and modern chairs, but his window framed a striking view: the temple's ancient stone carvings of dancing gods stood tall beside his computer's glowing code. His days followed a steady routine—fixing code between sips of strong office tea, attending meetings filled with tech terms like "scalability," while temple priests chanted nearby. Sometimes, he'd pause to stare at the temple's spire piercing the cloudy sky, wondering if Mounika in Bangalore ever looked at skyscrapers and thought of him.

Nights were livelier. The community centre buzzed with energy—its cracked walls covered in old movie posters, the air thick with sweat and determination. Here, Prem taught coding to underprivileged kids who typed furiously on second-hand keyboards, their eyes wide and eager as they learned. A girl named Riya, with messy braids and a patched uniform, once fixed a coding mistake he'd overlooked. *"Everything okay, sir?"* she asked, grinning at his surprise. In her pride, Prem saw his younger self—the boy who'd escaped poverty through math, now helping others do the same. The centre's lone fan spun noisily, stirring the sticky air as code lit up dusty screens. Every typed letter felt like a small act of defiance, a chance to rewrite their futures.

Evening sunlight streamed through dirty windows, casting long shadows over Riya as she bent over Prem's notebook. She pointed to an old drawing in the corner—a flock of birds' mid-flight, their wings smudged into the folds of the paper. *"Sir,"* she asked shyly, her voice quiet but curious, *"why do you always draw birds?"*

Prem stopped writing. He stared at the sketch—the rough, eager wings, as if they'd fought free from the page. Outside, temple bells rang for evening prayers, their sound mixing with his memories of Mounika's laugh. *"They remind me,"* he said softly, barely louder than the flickering lightbulb overhead, *"to keep flying, even when things are tough."*

A buzz broke the silence. His phone lit up the dim room: *"Mounika D. has viewed your profile."* The screen's glare revealed his shaky calm. His thumb froze—*Did she see his volunteer posts? The photo of him teaching near the temple?*—before he swiped it away. But in the quiet, he opened his contacts. There, saved under a name he'd never say out loud: *Wings.*

ᗞᗞᗞ

Bangalore overwhelmed Mounika—a chaotic city of honking auto-rickshaws spewing smoke, loud tech workers shouting on calls, and street sellers offering chai in cracked cups. Her hostel, hidden in a noisy part of the city, smelled of old, greasy curry and the harsh smell of disappointment. Her hostel room had peeled flower wallpaper and a creaky ceiling fan that spun weakly, doing nothing to cool the sticky heat. Job rejection emails woke her up at 3 a.m., their bright subject lines— *"We regret to inform you…"*—burning into the dark. Each rejection deepened the self-doubt Prabha had planted with cruel remarks like, *"You're lucky I tell the truth, Mona. Those kurtas make you look frumpy."*

Prabha's voice still reached her, but now as drunken late-night voicemails, drowned out by Bangalore's rain. *"Mishh you...."* Mounika deleted them, but guilt stuck in her throat like tar. Sometimes, she played them just to hear her old name—*Mona*—now as unfamiliar as the noisy city outside. The hostel's lone jasmine plant, a shrivelled stem in a rusty pot, shook in the wind, its dry soil proof it never belonged there.

In her dim room, Mounika flipped through her old, worn copy of *The God of Small Things*, its pages as fragile as her faded confidence. A dried jasmine sprig fell into her lap—Preethi's gift, forgotten between the book's pages. The petals turned to dust at her touch, scattering over a line where a character whispers, *"Don't be afraid."* The scent lingered—sandalwood, lemon candies, memories of Prem's hand brushing hers as he passed her a book. Her chest ached. Outside, rain battered the window, but the room felt crowded with ghosts.

At 2 a.m., bright neon lights from Bangalore's streets seeped through Mounika's thin curtain, staining her room pink and blue. Her phone burned in her hands as she typed *"I'm sorry"*—the blinking cursor daring her to send it. Outside, rain hissed on the hostel's tin roof, matching the chaos in her chest. She deleted the message, the apology vanishing into nothing, and slumped against the wall. Her sketchbook lay open to an unfinished drawing of a banyan tree, its roots twisting around two figures: one holding a dried jasmine, the other a smudged silver watch.

ᑭᑭᑭ

800 miles away, Prem stood on his balcony, the Lingaraj Temple's spire a dark shadow against the night sky. His jasmine plant sat stubbornly unbosomed; buds tightly closed. The city slept below, but Prem's mind raced. Riya had sent him a message—a screenshot of a simple game she'd fixed, with a pixelated bird flapping unevenly

across the screen. He'd sent a thumbs-up emoji, but his pride felt empty. Through his apartment window, he could see his office desk cluttered with relics of his past: a sticky note with half-written code (**"for i in range (2, 50):"**), a project he'd abandoned when Mounika left.

In Bangalore, Mounika's phone lit up—*"Prem K. has viewed your profile."* Her breath caught. Did he see her new bio? *Graphic designer. Looking for meaningful projects.* Or her post showcasing her wings sketch titled *"Flight Lessons"*? She clicked on his profile—his photo was the same: standing before the temple, smiling faintly, his eyes distant.

In Bhubaneswar, Prem's thumb hovered over her contact—**"Wings."** The balcony jasmine trembled in the wind, its leaves whispering secrets he couldn't decipher.

Prem's Desk: The sticky note curled at the edges, its code a monument to a love story coded in loops without end.

Mounika's Sketchbook: The banyan tree's roots now coiled around an empty space where a third figure might've stood—a ghostly outline, half-erased.

LinkedIn's Cold Logic: *"Viewed by Prem K. 2h ago." "Viewed by Mounika D. 5m ago."*

The jasmine bud split open at dawn, a single petal unfurling. Prem missed it, already at the community centre, where Riya's pixelated bird crashed into a firewall.

Mounika's charcoal snapped mid-stroke, the wing's tip veering off the page. Somewhere, the banyan tree sighed.

The rains followed Prem to Bhubaneswar.

The wings followed Mounika to Bangalore.

And somewhere, in the space between sent and unsent, their story refused to end.

New Winds and New Wings

It was a lazy Sunday morning, the kind where time dripped like honey. Mounika sat cross-legged on her bed, a steaming mug of coffee warming her palms. Sunlight spilled through the curtains, painting gold stripes on her freshly mopped floor. Her new job as a junior graphic designer had settled into a rhythm—respectful colleagues, a cubicle with a potted fern, and weekends blissfully free of Prabha's chaos. She'd just hung up a video call with her father, who'd fretted about her eating enough lentils, when a sharp knock rattled the door.

Mounika opened it to a vision.

The girl in the doorway was a storm of contradictions—wild curls the colour of monsoon soil tumbling over a neon-green crop top, eyes lined with kohl so sharp they could cut glass, and a smile that could've powered Bangalore's grid. Her denim jeans hugged curves that made the boys trip over their chai cups.

"Hey, I'm Mallika! call me Mini," she announced, hoisting a sequined duffel bag. "Your new roommate. Move, the universe demands a hug." Before Mounika could react, Mini engulfed her in a cloud of jasmine perfume and glitter.

Mini exploded into the room like confetti. She tossed her bag onto the empty bed, revealing a stash of nail polish, dog-eared romance novels, and a framed photo of a grinning old couple—her grandparents, she later explained. "So, spill!" she demanded, flopping onto Mounika's bed. "You're the quiet, artsy type, right? Let me guess—sketches tragic boys and writes poetry in Bengali?"

Mounika blinked. "Telugu, actually. And I don't write poe—"

"Close enough!" Mini laughed, her voice a melody that made even the flickering bulb seem brighter. She rummaged through her bag and tossed Mounika a *mango popsicle*. "Breakfast. Don't argue."

By noon, the room was a kaleidoscope of their lives. Mini's stories tumbled out—growing up in a Kerala fishing village, her MBA ("*Boring!*"), and her current gig as a fashion influencer

("*Basically, I get paid to be pretty*"). Mounika, usually guarded, found herself sharing snippets of her past—Prem, the banyan tree, the wings she still drew compulsively.

"*So, this Prem guy,*" Mini said, painting her toenails cherry red. "*He's, like, your tragic hero?*"

Mounika traced the rim of her coffee mug. "It's... *complicated.*"

"*Everything's complicated till you uncomplicate it.*" Mini winked. "*But first, let's fix your wardrobe. Those pyjamas scream 'I've given up on joy'.*"

Evening draped the city in purple shadows. They ordered *paneer biryani* and ate on the floor, legs tangled, sauce staining their fingertips. Mini's phone buzzed nonstop—DMs from her followers, she dismissed with eye rolls. "*Boys are like street dogs. Feed one, and fifty show up.*"

Mounika hesitated, then asked, "*Aren't you scared? Letting strangers...*"

"*Letting?*" Mini snorted. "*Honey, I don't let them. I exist, and they orbit. Their problem, not mine.*" She flicked biryani rice at Mounika. "*You should try it. Live a little.*"

Later, as Mini scrolled through Mounika's sketches, she paused at the half-finished banyan tree. "*This is him, isn't it?*" She tapped the smudged silver watch on the page.

Mounika nodded.

Mini grabbed her hand. "*Call him.*"

"*What? No, I—*"

"*Now.*" Mini thrust Mounika's phone into her palm. "*Before I hack your LinkedIn.*"

The phone rang once. Twice.

"*Hello?*"

Prem's voice—deeper now, roughened by distance—sent a shiver through her.

"*Hi. It's... me.*"

Silence. Then, softly, "*Mounika.*"

They talked. *Really* talked. About Mini's chaos, Riya's coding triumphs, the way Bhubaneswar's rains smelled different from

Bangalore's. No rushed goodbyes, no lurking shadows. When Prem laughed at her *paneer biryani* disaster story, Mounika realized her cheeks hurt from smiling.

"*I miss this,*" Prem said, the words tentative, like a bird testing its wings.

Outside, Mini whooped as she defeated a level on Candy Crush, her victory soundtrack to Mounika's quiet "*I miss it too.*"

▷▷▷

Mini sprawled across her bed, laptop balanced on her stomach, groaning. "*Why is coding so boring?*" She'd promised her followers a "*sexy tech guru*" video but was stuck editing a Python tutorial. "*Mouni, help! How do I make loops sound hot?*"

Mounika glanced up from her sketchbook. "*Loops are loops. They're not supposed to be hot.*"

"*Ugh, you're no fun.*" Mini tossed a sequined pillow at her. "*What if I wear glasses and a lab coat? Ooh, bad professor vibes—*"

"*Ask Prem,*" Mounika blurted, then froze.

Mini's eyes narrowed. "*Prem? Your Prem? The tragic banyan-tree guy?*"

Mounika's cheeks burned. "*He's a coder. He'll explain it... better.*"

Mini snatched Mounika's phone, grinning. "*Give me his number. Now.*"

Prem answered on the second ring; voice cautious. "*Hello?*"

"*Hey, hotshot! It's Mini—Mounika's roommate. I need coding magic.*"

Prem's confusion melted into laughter as Mini rambled. "*I need loops to sound spicy. Think... forbidden love in Python. Can you?*"

"*Forbidden love?*" Prem chuckled. "*Okay, let's try.*"

For an hour, he translated coding jargon into storytelling—variables as characters, loops as unresolved tension. Mini typed furiously, interjecting with "*Genius!*" and "*Wait, explain that kiss scene again!*"

Mounika pretended to sketch, ears catching Prem's voice—warmer, livelier than she'd heard in months.

"*You're a lifesaver, Prem!*" Mini sighed. "*Why's Mouni hiding you? You're gold.*"

A pause. "*She… she doesn't hide me.*"

"*Please. She sketches you daily but won't call. Drama queens, both of you.*"

Prem's breath hitched. "*She still draws me?*"

Mini winked at Mounika's panicked glare. "*Ask her yourself. Bye, SWEETHEART!*"

Mini tossed the phone back. "*He's into you. Like, coding-romance-novel into you.*"

Mounika stared at her half-finished sketch—Prem's watch, now tangled with Mini's cherry-red nails. "*Stop it.*"

"*No, listen.*" Mini knelt beside her. "*He kept asking about you. 'Does she still hate jasmine?' 'Is she eating?'*" She mimicked Prem's low, worried tone perfectly. "*He's a puppy. Adopt him.*"

Mounika's chest tightened. "*It's not that simple.*"

"*Because you're scared? Or because he might be?*" Mini snorted. "*You two and your tragic silence—it's exhausting.*"

That night, Mini's snores filled the room while Mounika replayed Prem's voice. "*She still draws me?*" Hope, raw and fragile, had cracked his words.

ᐯᐯᐯ

In Bhubaneswar, Prem paced his balcony, Mini's call echoing. "*Drama queens, both of you.*" He'd never admit how her boldness disarmed him—how she'd peeled open Mounika's world in minutes, a skill he'd failed to learn in years.

Riya's message buzzed: "*Fixed the bird game! Check attachment.*" The pixelated bird now soared smoothly, wings glitching no more. He typed, "*Proud of you,*" but his mind lingered on Mini's laugh, her effortless way of naming the unnamed.

Mounika's sketchbook page flickered in his memory—the watch, the wings. *She still draws me.*

He opened their chat, thumb hovering over the keyboard.

Prem:*Saw your wings post. They're… fearless.*

He deleted it.
Prem:*Mini's a hurricane.*
He sent it.

ᐅᐅᐅ

Mounika returned to the hostel, her arms full of grocery bags, and froze at the sound of Mini's laughter spilling into the corridor. Peering through the half-open door, she saw Mini sprawled on her bed, phone pressed to her ear, twirling a strand of hair around her finger.

"No way! You actually debugged it with that code? Prem, you're a genius!" Mini giggled, her toes painted neon pink kicking the air.

Mounika's grip tightened on the bags. She recognized that tone—the one Mini used when flirting with admirers. Quietly, she retreated to the common kitchen, her coffee forgotten. The jasmine plant on the windowsill trembled as she passed, its lone bud still clenched shut.

ᐅᐅᐅ

Later, Mini sat cross-legged on her bed, editing a vlog about *"coding for beginners."* Her screen blurred as her mind wandered to Prem's voice earlier—patient, amused, *interested*. She opened their chat, typing:
Mini:*Still owe you for the coding help. Drinks?*
She deleted it.
Mini:*Mouni's out. Call if you're free.*
Deleted again.

"Ugh!" She threw her phone aside, spotting Mounika's sketchbook peeking from under the pillow. The pages revealed Prem's watch, now entwined with wings. Mini traced the lines, guilt knotting her stomach.

ᐅᐅᐅ

In Bhubaneswar, Prem stared at Mounika's latest Instagram post—a sketch of a storm cloud pierced by sunlight. He typed a comment, erased it, then messaged her:

Prem:*The cloud sketch... it's different. Bold.*

Minutes passed. No reply.

His phone buzzed—**Mini:***Need help again. SOS, nerd!*

He called, relieved when her laughter flooded the line. They dissected her coding script, but the conversation veered to Mounika.

"She's been... quiet," Prem ventured.

"She's always quiet," Mini said lightly. *"But her sketches scream. You should see the new one."*

Prem's chest ached. *She shares more with you than me.*

ᚦᚦᚦ

One evening, Mini video-called Prem, Mounika reluctantly squeezed into the frame.

"Group project!" Mini declared, winking. *"Mouni's designing my new channel logo. Prem, rate her draft!"*

Mounika's sketch flashed on screen—a bird mid-flight, its wings a mosaic of code snippets.

"It's... incredible," Prem said softly.

Mounika mumbled thanks, eyes darting away.

Mini's grin faltered. *"Okay, awkward silence over! Prem, tell us your worst date story."*

As Prem recounted a college mishap, Mini laughed too loudly. Mounika excused herself, claiming a work email.

Later, Mini found her on the rooftop, hugging her knees.

"You okay?"

"Just tired," Mounika lied, watching a plane vanish into the clouds.

Mini sat beside her, their shoulders brushing. *"He misses you, you know."*

Mounika's silence screamed louder than words.

ᚦᚦᚦ

That night, Prem replayed the call in his thoughts. Mounika's avoidance. Mini's forced cheer. *Why does this feel familiar?*

Riya's game update glowed on his laptop—the bird now crashed if players hesitated too long. *"Fear makes it fall,"* she'd explained.

He opened Mounika's chat, typing:

Prem:*We need to talk. About us. About everything.*

He deleted it.

Prem:*The bird in your sketch… does it ever land?*

He hit send.

ᐅᐅᐅ

Mounika's life became a blur of office parties and weekend brunches with her new colleagues—a lively group of designers who joked about deadlines and swapped Spotify playlists. Her cubicle, once cluttered with sketchbooks, now held client mood boards and coffee cups emblazoned with startup logos. When Prem called, she let it ring out, texting later: *"Swamped. Talk soon?"*

But *"soon"* never came.

One evening, as her colleagues debated rooftop bars, Mounika's phone lit up—**Mini:***Prem's asking about you. Call him?* She silenced it, laughing too loudly at a joke she hadn't heard.

ᐅᐅᐅ

Mini sat cross-legged on her bed, her laptop glowing with a video call. Prem's face filled the screen, his brow furrowed as he debugged her latest coding tutorial.

"You're a lifesaver," Mini said, twirling her hair. *"Seriously, what would I do without you?"*

Prem shrugged. *"Crash and burn, probably."*

They laughed, but the silence that followed hummed with something unspoken.

"Prem…" Mini hesitated, her playful mask slipping. *"I… I like you. Like, really like you."*

The screen froze—not from Wi-Fi, but from Prem's stillness.

"Mini…"

"You don't have to say anything!" she rushed, cheeks flaming. *"I just… needed you to know."*

Prem's voice softened. *"I care about you. A lot. But not... not like that."*

Mini nodded, her smile brittle. *"Yeah. Yeah, I figured."*

ᐯᐯᐯ

The hostel room felt colder after the call. Mini scrolled through Prem's messages—jokes, coding tips, *"Check this song!"*—now tinted with loss. She opened Mounika's drawer, eyeing the half-finished banyan tree sketch.

Why does it still hurt?

When Mounika stumbled in hours later, Mini pretended to sleep.

ᐯᐯᐯ

In Bhubaneswar, Prem stared at Riya's latest game update. The pixelated bird now had two paths—*Fly North* or *Fly South*.

"Players hate choosing," Riya had said. *"But they have to."*

He opened Mini's chat, typing apologies, explanations, deleting them all. His heart ached for her laughter, her light—but not her heart.

His phone buzzed—**Mounika:***Saw your comment on my post. Thanks.*

He replied instantly: *"The wings... they're different. Freer."*

No response.

Weeks passed.

Mini's vlogs grew quieter, her neon nails chipped. Prem buried himself in work, coding late to avoid his empty balcony. Mounika's sketches turned abstract—storms without birds, watches without hands.

One rainy night, Mini found Mounika crying in the stairwell, her phone open to Prem's old messages.

"You miss him," Mini said, not a question.

Mounika wiped her face. *"It's too late."*

Mini sat beside her, their shoulders touching. *"It's never too late to fix your bugs."*

ᐯᐯᐯ

At dawn, Prem sent a voice note: *"Mounika, I'm coming to Bangalore. We need to talk. Please."*

The jasmine plant on her windowsill trembled, its bud finally cracking open—one petal unfurling, fragile and white.

A new story begins

The plane's wheels screeched against Bengaluru's tarmac, the sound slicing through Prem's restless thoughts. Stepping into the city's humid embrace felt like walking into a sauna—sticky, suffocating, alive. Auto-rickshaws swarmed like hornets outside the airport, their drivers hollering offers in a cacophony of Kannada and broken English. Prem clutched his duffel bag tighter, the weight of his purpose pressing heavier than the luggage.

He checked into a hotel on Church Street, its glass façade reflecting the chaos of the city. The room was sterile—cream walls, a queen bed with stiff linens, and a desk cluttered with pamphlets for tech park tours. He tossed his bag onto the floor, the *thud* echoing in the silence.

For two days, Prem's phone became an extension of his hand. He called her at dawn, noon, midnight—each time met with the same response of not getting answered. Texts piled up in her inbox like unread poetry:

Day 1: *"I'm here. Let's talk. Please."*
Day 2: *"Mounika, just tell me you're okay."*
Day 3: *"..."*

By the fourth day, he stopped. The hotel room smelled of recycled AC and loneliness. Room service trays stacked up—cold dosas, untouched coffee, a wilting jasmine sprig the waiter had tucked beside his cutlery.

One evening, Prem stood at the floor-to-ceiling window, watching monsoon rain lash the streets below. His phone buzzed—a LinkedIn notification. **Mounika D. has viewed your profile.** He hurled the device onto the bed, the screen cracking like the fragile hope he'd carried here.

ᐳᐳᐳ

The hotel room stank of stagnation—stale coffee, wilted jasmine, and the sour tang of hopelessness. Prem lay on the bed, staring at the ceiling, his phone clutched like a dead weight in his hand. Four days of calls. Four days of texts. Four days of silence. The screen glared back at him with Mounika's last Instagram post: a blurry train window, captioned *"Goodbye, Bengaluru."*

He didn't hear the first buzz.

Mini:*Prem. Answer me.*

His thumb hovered over her name. He typed, deleted, typed again:

Prem:*She's gone. Just... gone.*

Mini's reply was instant, her words sharp with urgency:

Mini:*I know. She left for her hometown. Didn't tell anyone, not even me. Are you okay?*

Prem's laugh cracked the silence—a hollow, broken sound. He threw the phone. It skidded across the floor, the screen shattering like the last shred of his resolve.

ÞÞÞ

The truth coiled around him, venomous and suffocating. *She left. Without a word. Without him.* He paced the room, fists clenched, replaying every unanswered call, every unread text. The jasmine sprig on the nightstand—once fragrant, now brittle—crumbled under his trembling grip.

When the anger burned out, numbness seeped in. He slid to the floor, back against the bed, eyes fixed on the fractured phone screen. Mini's messages lit up the darkness:

Mini:*Prem. Please.*

Mini:*Let me come over.*

Mini:*Don't shut me out.*

He didn't reply. Couldn't. The walls felt closer; the air thinner.

ÞÞÞ

Hours later, his phone buzzed again. This time, a voice note. Her voice—soft, frayed at the edges—cut through the fog: *"Meet me. Tomorrow. Cubbon Park, near the statue. Please."*

Prem pressed replay. Then again. And again. Her words tangled with the hum of the AC, the drip of the broken bathroom tap, the echo of his own ragged breath.

On the floor, the jasmine's ghostly scent still lingered.

ᐅᐅᐅ

Mini stood in front of her full-length mirror, the morning sun spilling through her hostel window and pooling like liquid gold around her feet. She had spent hours curating this look—every detail deliberate, every choice a quiet rebellion against the ache of unspoken feelings.

Her white cotton t-shirt clung to her frame like a second skin, the fabric soft yet unforgiving in how it traced the curves of her upper body. She paired it with high-waisted blue jeans, faded at the knees and tailored to perfection. The denim embraced her legs like a sculptor's final touch, accentuating the gentle flare of her hips and the lean taper of her thighs. On her feet, white canvas sneakers gleamed, pristine and effortless, as if she'd stepped straight out of a sunlit ad campaign.

Her hair, usually tamed into braids or ponytails, cascaded freely down her back in waves of chestnut silk. Her makeup was minimal but intentional: a dusting of rose-tinted blush to highlight the apples of her cheeks, mascara that deepened the espresso richness of her lashes, and light pink lipstick that glazed her lips with a dewy, bitten-berry sheen.

Mini turned sideways, studying her reflection. The t-shirt pulled slightly at her midsection, outlining her stomach. Her jeans emphasized the hourglass arc of her silhouette, a harmony of curves and angles that felt both powerful and vulnerable.

This is me, she thought, meeting her own gaze in the mirror. *Not hiding, not pretending.*

As she stepped out, the red handbag swayed at her hip, a beacon in the Bangalore haze. The white shoes tapped rhythmically against the pavement, each step a quiet anthem of resolve. She didn't just look beautiful—she looked *alive*, a collision of grace and grit, every inch of her radiating the kind of magnetism that turned sidewalks into runways and strangers into admirers.

But this wasn't for them.

It was for the boy who'd once called her *"hurricane"* with a smile, and for the girl in the mirror who'd finally stopped running from her own reflection.

ᚥᚥᚥ

Cubbon Park breathed in the golden-hour light, the air thick with the musk of rain-damp earth and the sweet rot of fallen champak blossoms. Prem and Mini sat on a weathered teak bench, its wood grooved with decades of lovers' initials and lost promises. Between them lay a paper bag of roasted peanuts, untouched.

Mini had chosen this spot deliberately—the champak tree behind them, its branches heavy with creamy, star-shaped flowers, their perfume cloying and relentless. *Like hope*, she thought bitterly.

They'd talked about Mounika for exactly fifty-three minutes. Prem's voice had been a dull blade, sawing through the same questions: *Why did she leave? Did she mention me? Does she hate me?* Mini answered in monosyllables, her nails digging crescents into her palms.

Now, as the sun bled into the horizon, Mini turned to him. Her red handbag glowed like a wound against the bench.

"Enough about her," she said, too brightly. *"What about us?"*

Prem stiffened. His gaze stayed fixed on a troop of langurs scrambling in the distance. *"Mini…"*

"No, listen." She shifted, her white sneakers brushing his scuffed loafers. The pink gloss on her lips caught the dying light. *"We're good together. You make me laugh. I make you… less broody. We could try. Really try."*

A breeze stirred the champak blooms. One landed in Prem's hair. Mini resisted the urge to pluck it out.

He finally looked at her, his eyes red-rimmed, his stubble a shadow he'd stopped caring to shave. *"You deserve more than a half-dead man, Mini."*

The words hung between them, blunt and bruising.

Mini's laugh was a shattered thing. "*You think I don't know that?*" She leaned closer, her jasmine perfume clashing with the champak's sweetness. "*But I'd rather have halves of you than wholes of anyone else.*"

Prem's hand twitched toward hers, then retreated. "*I can't,*" he whispered. "*Not when every part of me still belongs to her.*"

The rejection wasn't a surprise. Still, it carved through her like a scalpel.

For a long moment, they sat in silence. The langurs screeched. A street vendor's radio wailed an old Kishore Kumar song.

Then Mini did something extraordinary—she smiled.

"*Okay,*" she said, straightening her spine. The red handbag slid into her lap like a shield. "*Okay.*"

Prem frowned. "*Okay?*"

"*You're a mess. She's a mess. I'm...*" She gestured to her flawless outfit, the irony not lost on her. "*...this. But you're stuck with me, got it? No more hiding in hotel rooms. We're getting dosa tonight. And you're paying.*"

Prem's laugh was rusty, disbelieving. "*You're insane.*"

"*And you're buying me extra chutney.*" She stood, slinging the red bag over her shoulder. "*Up. Now.*"

He rose, his movements sluggish, but his shoulders lighter. As they walked, Mini's hand brushed his—once, twice—before she linked their pinkies. She just pressed herself against him touching his lips with hers'. He didn't move away. He didn't want to. He let her kiss him and pull him out. After what he called an eternity, he looked into her eyes and she winked at him. Like nothing happened, she held his palm and started walking.

ᛈᛈᛈ

Time had softened the edges of Prem's heartache. Mounika's absence, once a gaping wound, had scarred over, leaving only faint echoes of what once was. He no longer traced her name in the margins of his notebooks or startled at the ping of a notification.

Her memory had become a distant star, its light dimmed by the sunrise of Mini's laughter.

Mini's love was not a storm but a steady rain, gentle and life-giving. She did not erase the past; she rewrote it. In her, Prem found the courage to mend—not by forgetting, but by choosing to breathe anew. Her hands, once painted cherry-red to mask her fears, now held his without trembling. Her words, once sharp and unfiltered, now wove stories of shared tomorrows.

One evening, as they sat beneath the champak tree in Cubbon Park, its petals drifting like confetti, Prem realized he could no longer recall the exact shade of Mounika's eyes. Instead, he saw Mini's—warm, unguarded, alive with a future he'd stopped fearing.

"*Thank you,*" he murmured, pressing a Champa blossom into her palm.

"*For what?*" she asked, though her smile already knew.

"*For being the escape, I didn't know I needed... and the home I'll never leave.*"

The breeze carried away the last fragments of a love once lost, leaving only the quiet certainty of a love newly found.

In the garden of his heart, winter's frost thawed to spring.
Where Mounika's silence had sown shadows,
Mini's laughter grew gardens.
Her love, a compass in the wreckage,
Led him not to forgetting,
But to rebirth.
And in her eyes,
He found the wings
To finally let go and fly away!!!

Epilogue

Love is never truly lost. It lingers in the unspoken words, in the memories that refuse to fade, and in the quiet spaces between heartbeats. The stories in this book are not just tales of love and separation—they are echoes of emotions we have all felt at some point in our lives.

As I wrote these stories, I realized that love, in its purest form, never really ends. It transforms, it waits, and sometimes, it finds its way back in the most unexpected ways. Whether through a chance meeting, an unbroken promise, or the silent understanding between two souls, love continues to weave its own destiny. Some of the scenes in the book are real life experiences of my friends and some strangers I met, who shared them. Some made me cry and some made me re-think the purpose of emotions in our lives. They made me understood the preferences that we should choose to lead happy and peaceful days, everyday. Love is important but we should love ourselves first in order to love someone else. A soul that doesn't know how to love itself can never love another.

Each story I wrote in this book had been felt very deeply. "Between two heartbeats" is narrated by my wife. She's an aspiring dancer. She loves to dance so she narrated the story of a dancer who fell in love with a poet. Her imagination is simple but strong. The emotions in the pages were just felt and written.

If these stories have stirred even a single emotion within you, if they have reminded you of a lost love, a cherished moment, or the hope of finding love again, then this book has served its purpose.

Thank you for allowing me to share these emotions with you. And remember—every love story, no matter how lost it may seem, is simply waiting for its next chapter.

With warmth and gratitude,
Sarath Kumar

Author's Note

Writing *Some Lost Stories* has been an emotional journey—one filled with love, longing, and hope on the many ways we connect and disconnect in life. These stories are not just works of fiction; they are fragments of emotions, whispers of memories, and echoes of the love we have all experienced in some form.

As a writer, I have always believed that words have the power to make us feel, to transport us to a different time and place, and to remind us of the moments we hold dear. While writing these stories, I found inspiration in the real-life experiences of people I met—some were strangers who entrusted me with their untold emotions, while others were friends who shared pieces of their past. Their stories, their joys, and their heartbreaks found a place within these pages. With their permission, I have woven fragments of their lives into these narratives, blending reality with fiction to create something heartfelt and true.

If these stories have touched your heart, made you smile, or even brought a tear to your eye, then I consider my purpose fulfilled.

Your time, your emotions, and your connection to these stories mean more than words can express.

Some Lost Stories - About The Book

Some Lost Stories is a collection of three deeply emotional love stories, each centred around the theme of losing and rediscovering love. The book takes readers on a journey through the lives of characters who experience heartbreak, separation, and the pain of lost connections. Yet, through fate, time, or sheer determination, love finds its way back into their lives in unexpected ways.

Each story explores different shades of love—whether it's a romance that was never meant to end, a love that resurfaces after years of distance, or a bond that remains unbroken despite life's challenges. With rich storytelling and heartfelt emotions, *Some Lost Stories* beautifully captures the essence of longing, hope, and the belief that true love never really fades—it just waits to be found again

About The Author

I, Sarath Kumar Kalamata am a writer and storyteller who finds inspiration in the world around me. A former web developer turned writer, I have always been drawn to the power of words and the emotions they carry. I got my inspiration from an early age when I first read poetry during my school days. Since then, reading became one of my favorite hobbies.

I enjoy spending time in nature, riding along serene beaches, and going on long bike rides. More than anything, I cherishes the moments spent with my friends and family, especially with my daughter.

My writings are deeply rooted in my observations and emotions, shaped by the simple yet profound moments of life. From the silent whispers of the wind to the untold stories in a stranger's eyes, everything around me fuels my creative spirit.

My previous book, ***Waves of Heart: An Anthology of Short Stories***, was a collection of poems that explored love, loss, and the many shades of human emotions. With ***Some Lost Stories***, I continue my journey of storytelling, weaving tales of love, loss, and the beauty of second chances.

Contact me through the social channels mentioned below and let me know your views on my books.

fb/@WavesOfHeart

ig/@sarathwrites

Thank you!!

Waves of Heart: An Anthology of Short Poems

Waves of Heart is a soulful collection of poems and short stories that explore the depths of love, longing, and human emotions. Through beautifully crafted words, the book takes readers on a journey through the many shades of life—happiness, heartbreak, hope, and healing.

Each poem and story in this anthology is a reflection of the emotions we all experience but often struggle to put into words. Inspired by real moments, heartfelt observations, and the world around us, Waves of Heart captures the raw beauty of relationships, the passage of time, and the silent emotions that shape our lives.